GRATITUDE OPENS
THE DOOR

Five Generations of a Faith-Filled Family

Mary Ann B. Fontenot

To my precious children,
Greg, Amy, and Matthew,

Raising you has been a joy,
a privilege, and my greatest accomplishment.

All my love,
Mom

Table of Contents

Acknowledgements

First and foremost, I would like to thank God for His luminous and magnanimous friendship, for giving me a second chance at life, for my many blessings, and for entrusting me with the task of giving testimony to His power and glory.

I especially want to thank Amanda Barry, my typist, sounding board, confidante, personal assistant, and friend, who has been with me on this journey every step of the way. Together, we have met self-imposed deadlines, critiqued my writing, and traded really bad "Dad jokes" along the way. I never could have accomplished this enormous endeavor without you.

Hearty thanks go to my dad, Stanley, and to my three children, Greg, Amy, and Matthew, for providing all the humor in the book.

Thank you to my brother, Lou Bridges, for being there for me, day or night. You've been my friend, my adviser, and my go-to medical expert.

Many thanks to my nearest and dearest friend, Liz Brinkhaus Padgett, for your gifts of endless patience, extraordinary faith, and selfless love that helped me to become a better person and molded me into the woman I am today.

To my dear Sr. Marie Louise, thanks to you and all the wonderful Sisters of the Covington Carmelite Monastery for praying for me daily throughout this powerful yearlong journey.

To Dr. Ken Spiller, thank you for keeping me alive and well for the last ten years. You are a brilliant diagnostician and have continued to unravel the mystery that is my body, post cancer. You and your nurse, Keisha, have earned my utmost respect and gratitude.

A big thank you goes to Susan Castille who provided valuable guidance and necessary encouragement from the beginning.

My fondest appreciation to my "editor-in-chief" and precious daughter-in-law, Rebecca Padgett Fontenot, and to my dear friend, Rosie Zehnder, for spending countless hours refining my work.

Thanks also to my son, Greg Fontenot, and my friends, Mitzi Domino, Anne Calhoun, and Phil Bertrand, for their editorial contributions, and to Tiny Dugas for her research on my genealogy.

And to all of those special friends who have been praying for me over the years, thank you for your faithfulness, your support, and most of all your love.

Introduction

My brief encounter with the Living God was so vivid that the rest of my extraordinary life pales in comparison. – May 15, 1993

This book started as a labor of love for my children. Being a twenty-six year cancer survivor, I had already beaten the odds, but my fourth near-death experience left me wanting to write down all my family's history and stories while I still had the chance. Realizing that I could perhaps touch lives far beyond my own family, I began to write with a renewed purpose. My hope is that I can encourage, entertain, educate, empower, and enlighten readers along the way!

For many years – a couple of decades actually – I avoided writing my story. People told me more often than I can count that I should write a book, but I was paralyzed by fear – fear of failure, fear of rejection, and fear of embarrassment. You name it, I was afraid of it. In the end, God gave me no option *but* to write, and through Scripture readings at Mass, He inspired and encouraged me along my journey. Finally, I understood that my story was not about *me* at all, it was about *God*. Once I got that, I was free to write. Enjoy these stories from a bygone era!

The cover art, painted by Lyn Hill, is a watercolor of Leo and Carmelite LeBlanc's house built in the mid 1920s. My brother Lou and I commissioned this painting of our grandparents' home as a gift to our mother, shortly after her father died. Today, it hangs over the piano in my home.

Chapter One

The News

How could something so painful bring about so much good?

I remember the exact moment when my life changed dramatically. It was a bright, sunny, August day full of hope and optimism as my husband Jeff and I walked into the doctor's office. We were there to discover the results of a biopsy of a mouth ulcer I had on my tongue. The ulcer appeared innocent enough at the beginning, but after it stubbornly refused to go away, I was forced to take action.

Honestly, I expected (or perhaps wished) the doctor to say something like, "Oh, Mrs. Fontenot, it's a simple mouth ulcer. Use this magic mouth wash three times a day and in a week, it will be gone! Poof!" But I was deluding myself, and the news hit me like a sucker punch from a close friend – hard and unexpected. It was actually the nurse who delivered the blow, those fateful words which forever changed my life, "You've got cancer."

At that point I went into a fog. You see, I had never even considered cancer because things like that don't happen to me. That's a disease that affects other people. After all I was only thirty-three years old, exercised religiously, never smoked a day in my life, and rarely drank alcohol. My diet was so healthy that bran was one of my four major food groups! How could this be?

When I got home, the walls of fear and denial starting closing in on me, so I quickly fell to my knees and prayed more intensely than I had ever prayed in my life. I felt so close to the Lord that it seemed we were one being. Perhaps we were all along.

Poked, prodded, and punctured, my body marched through a battery of tests and physical examinations; however, my spirit soared as it became one with Christ in His agony. To someone who has never experienced it, it may be hard to understand the ecstasy of realizing just how important we are to God and the joy of discovering how much Jesus really cares about us. In that moment, I felt personally and deeply loved by the Creator of the Universe. At the time, it was all new to me. Now it is quite familiar.

Travel with me now as I take you on the journey of my life and personal encounters with the very presence of God. In the summer of 1992, I was sailing high on the cruise ship of life. Happily married to a man named Jeff, I was the mother of three beautiful children, Greg who was six, Amy who was four, and

Matthew who was five months old. I had a fulfilling job as a pharmacist, a variety of interests, and many friends. To me, my abrupt and completely unexpected diagnosis of advanced tongue cancer sounded very much like a death sentence. It was as if I had suddenly fallen overboard into the dark, murky waters of the unknown.

I was thirty-three years old and had assumed that I was in the middle of my life; however, I quickly realized that this could be the end. All of the hopes, plans, and dreams I had for a bright and exciting future came to a screeching halt as I simply struggled to survive, one day at a time. While I tried to make sense of this bizarre situation in which I was suddenly immersed, God made His presence known loud and clear. Some might call it a coincidence, but I like to think of it as a God-incidence.

The day after I learned that I had cancer, my only sibling Lou, a medical doctor and assistant professor at University of Alabama at Birmingham, was taking four young residents on rounds with him. Lou had been teaching them for thirty days and this was their last day. Wracked with grief as a brother and feeling helpless as a physician, Lou arrived to make rounds completely frazzled.

"I'm sorry guys. I'm not worth much today. My only sister was diagnosed with cancer, and I was up all night trying to figure out a way to help her."

One of the young residents, Dr. Paul Goepfert, asked, "What kind of cancer does she have?"

"Tongue cancer" Lou replied.

Astoundingly, Paul said, "My dad is Professor and Chairman of the Department of Head and Neck Surgery at M.D. Anderson Cancer Center in Houston. I'll go give him a call."

I've heard it said that when God closes a door, He opens a window. Just as quickly as that door figuratively slammed shut, a window burst open bringing in the light! I have one brother, and Lou only had four students, and then, just for thirty days; my diagnosis fell at the last possible moment.

At the time, the young man's father, Dr. Helmuth Goepfert, was widely considered to be the best head and neck cancer surgeon and leading researcher in America, perhaps even the world. I firmly believe that because of his expertise, I am alive twenty-six years after my initial diagnosis. I thank God daily that I was given the extra time to raise my children.

The morning of my surgery, I remember laying on the gurney in total fear. I was scared because they were going to cut out part of my tongue, and as a pharmacist, being able to speak and counsel people was part of my livelihood. All I could think of in that moment was the Bible verse Jeff had taught me "Trust in the Lord with all your heart, and lean not unto your own understanding. In all your ways acknowledge Him, and He will direct your paths" (Proverbs 3:5-6). As I repeated that proverb to myself, I felt a calmness come over me as if I'd had a Valium.

Jeff's parents were kind enough to watch the children so that he could be in Houston with me and my parents for the surgery. A few days later, when our first grader, Greg, asked his Dad to take him to a meeting at school to sign up for cub scouts, Jeff drove four hours home, took Greg to the meeting, and then drove back to Houston the next morning. Jeff was such a loving and thoughtful man; he would go to the ends of the earth for his family.

After my surgery and five days in the hospital, Jeff took me to my parents' home in Covington where I could rest and recuperate a few more days without the rambunctious little ones. My mom in particular nurtured me through that time. One example was when she cut up a banana and brought it to me in a beautiful bowl, saying, "I didn't want you to have to expend your energy peeling that banana. Now all you have to do is eat it up." Realizing there was nothing she could do to help me physically, Mom bolstered me emotionally. I felt such bountiful love in that moment and I have never forgotten it.

Mom also encouraged me when I was down. She wisely told me, "Just because you make plans for your death doesn't mean you're going to die, anymore than making plans for your life means you're going to live." The more I pondered that, the more I realized its truth. That allowed me put my affairs in order without feeling hopeless or depressed.

Recently, I came across a letter I had written twenty-six years ago to Mom and Dad prior to my stay. I wrote, "I won't be able to speak much because when I talk too much, I bite my tongue and the sides of my mouth until they bleed." I continued, "God is using me as an instrument in this matter and I may not fully know why for years, but I love Him all the same. If it is the Lord's will, this will be a brief three to four week episode in a long and happy life. If not, He'll give me the strength to deal with whatever comes up." And indeed He did. That was written in September of 1992. God is so good! I'm such a fan!

Fortunately, I was in good shape before I was diagnosed with cancer, and as a result was able to get back into my exercise routine a month after the surgery. Life went on pretty much like it had before. I was too optimistic and naïve to even consider that the cancer might come back, which is probably a good thing. That first cancer episode left me with a long scar on my neck, which I like to call my red badge of courage, and *way* too much pride for my own good. That, however, would change dramatically in a few short months.

One night, five months later, my friend Liz and I had gone to the "picture show." After the movie, I asked Liz, "Feel my neck. Do you feel a lump?" She said, "Maybe? Barely though. I really can't tell." Well, within two weeks that imperceptible lump had grown to the size of a walnut. With fear and dread, I made an appointment to see Dr. Goepfert. A week later, I was in the operating room. Upon awakening from what was supposed to be a complicated, eight-hour surgery involving two different surgeons, I realized that only an hour had gone by on the clock. My heart sank.

Examining Dr. Goepfert's face closely, I asked, "It was supposed to be an eight-hour surgery, but it has only been an hour. What did you see when you opened me up? Am I going to die?"

I remember distinctly that he paused before answering, choosing his words very carefully before saying in his thick, German accent, "I think it is still curable at this time."

Brilliant! His words were brilliant! They left room for hope. They didn't present the odds, which surely must have been gloomy and disheartening. To this day, I am grateful to Dr. Helmuth Goepfert for his efforts in saving my life.

After my second surgery, we learned that the cancer had spread to my lymph nodes, on its way to the brain, lungs, or liver. At that point in time, patients were normally directed to wait four weeks before starting the painful radiation treatments, so they could heal a bit from the surgery before the area was burned. However, my cancer was very aggressive which meant I didn't have the luxury of time. I was given only two weeks to recover before radiation began in order to have a fighting chance against the quickly spreading cancer.

My radiation oncologist, Dr. Robert S. Fields at Mary Bird Perkins Cancer Center in Baton Rouge, warned me that during radiation, the pain would increase steadily as my flesh was burned layer by layer in an effort to kill the cancer cells. He also told me I should double my caloric intake, but insisted that it would be harder than it sounded. *Hmm*, I thought. *I've never had trouble overeating before.* Dr. Fields continued, telling me that I would lose my taste buds, my salivary glands would dry up, I would be nauseated all the time, and I would be in intense pain. *Well! That kind of put a damper on things!* How ironic. Like many people, I have battled weight problems most of my life, and wouldn't you know it? The one time a doctor gave me – not only his permission – but his blessing to eat everything in sight, I could barely taste, much less swallow!

My tongue was burned so deeply that even eating a single pancake was time consuming and painful; I lost weight rapidly. Weak and dehydrated after only the first ten days of treatments, I didn't have the strength to walk into the building; Jeff had to get a wheel chair. The doctor suggested I get a feeding tube put in my stomach for nutrition, which I tell people is like getting shot with a gun, but having the bullet only go halfway through your body. I have only two words for that: not fun.

Every day became a struggle to survive. The waves of pain and fear threatened to submerge me at any moment. I became so desperately ill that Jeff and I made plans for my life insurance money to continue our children's education. I even took the precaution of asking my best friend, Liz, to mother my children after I was gone. Jeff was a good man and I knew my boys would be fine, but I worried about Amy. Who would make sure she had Christmas dress? Who would teach her how to braid her hair? Who would take her to the ballet? Jeff would not think of those things. It was a heartbreaking experience.

For the first time, I truly embraced the words that I had repeated so often in the Our Father, "Thy will be done." I finally got it. It's not *my* will be done, it's *Thy* will be done. On that day, I gave God complete control of my mind, heart, and spirit, willingly accepting the fact that, like it or not, my death might be imminent. My faith had never been stronger. At that very moment of acceptance of God's sovereignty over my life, I felt peace spread through my body like a sip of hot chocolate on a cold winter's night. I was thirty-three years old and dying, the oldest of my three children was in the first grade, and I had never felt more at peace with life.

Throughout the first four weeks of radiation, the excruciating pain continued to worsen. Tolerating two more weeks of this was unimaginable. It was the night of Good Friday, 1993. I couldn't sleep a wink, pacing the floor all night in agony. Saturday brought another pain wracked day and sleepless night, leaving me at the end of my rope. On Easter Sunday I couldn't stand it any longer. I called my doctor and he changed my pain medicine to morphine; I was finally able to drift off to sleep.

The next morning I woke up vomiting violently. It was bright green. I wondered if this was what dying felt like. Jeff took off of work to drive me to Baton Rouge; if I was dying that day, he wanted to be with me. We soon found out that the vomiting had occurred as a side effect of the morphine. I was devastated, fearing that without morphine, the excruciating pain and sleepless nights would return.

Incredibly, from that day forward the pain diminished, even without the morphine. There was such a dramatic difference in my pain level that the following day I asked Dr. Fields if he had lowered my radiation dosage.

He replied calmly, "Nothing has changed."

I was stunned! I asked him why he thought the pain diminished after only four weeks, when he had told me it would increase steadily every day for six weeks.

His response was one that I will never forget, "*I have no medical explanation for that.*"

I've always heard that God will never give you more than you can handle. I firmly believe that on that day, God took my pain away. Our God is a loving, caring, awe-inspiring Father who is personally involved in our lives to the extent that we invite Him to be. And believe you me, I was on my knees inviting Him on a daily basis!

Now, let me tell you *my experience* of Jesus while I was sick. After the first ten days of radiation, I was too weak to care for my own children. Jeff was working overtime to pay for our mounting bills while his mother moved in with us to help take care of the children. She stayed six weeks, away from her husband and her home, her church and her friends. *Jesus volunteers.* A neighbor that I had never met before, Mimi Anderson, pulled over a wagon filled with pork chops, rice and gravy, corn on the cob and bread, strawberries, cake and whipped topping for our whole family. *Jesus caters.* My youngest child's first birthday came right when I was the sickest, and I was worried that my little Matthew would miss having his first birthday party. Well not one, but two different friends threw surprise birthday parties for him, complete with party hats, blowers, cake, and ice cream. *Jesus parties.* My friend Mitzi Domino brought a gift and some cinnamon rolls to cheer me up. *Jesus visits.* Every friend who sent flowers or came over to encourage me was a life jacket in the murky waters of my existence, giving me just enough hope to make it through one more day. *Jesus cares.* I received over 250 cards and letters from family, friends, acquaintances and strangers, the farthest away being from a priest in Sri Lanka. (I didn't even know where Sri Lanka was! I had to look it up on a map.) *Jesus writes.* Daily for six weeks, one of a half dozen friends took three hours out of their day to drive me back and forth to Baton Rouge for radiation treatments. *Jesus taxis.*

All of these people were Jesus to me, coming to my aid when I so desperately needed it, truly living His words ... "Love your neighbor as yourself." Jesus Christ is alive and well and living in my neighborhood. Do I believe in Jesus Christ? ABSOLUTELY! I have encountered Him many times.

At the beginning of my treatments, Dr. Fields had informed me that if the cancer returned, there was nothing else he could do. After my radiation ended, I went into a deep depression. To help me deal with this quicksand of emotion I was experiencing, I turned to my beloved church, Holy Cross Catholic Church. Dale LeBlanc, the Director of Religious Education, was there that fateful day and walked with me to the empty, darkened church, where she prayed aloud for me. Then she left me kneeling alone to pray.

I talked to God, basically pleading with Him for my life. To this day, I still remember my prayer: "God, I've lived a good life, and I'm okay with dying, but these *children,* Lord! *Please don't leave my children motherless.*"

Sitting down in the pew, I picked up a hymnal and randomly flipped through the more than 900 songs. The book came to rest on number 435, a song called <u>Sing to the Mountains</u>. My eyes were instantly drawn halfway down the page to the words, "I will give thanks to you my Lord. You have answered my plea. You have saved my soul from death." The thought "*YOU WILL NOT DIE*" instantly branded itself in my mind. I still get chills thinking about it. It could not have been more apparent that God was speaking directly to me. I remember it like it was yesterday. In that moment, my mission in life became crystal clear. It was two-fold: to be a fierce lioness of a mother raising my children to love and serve the Lord, and to give my testimony at every opportunity possible. My depression cleared instantly, and I began to enjoy life again.

Never one to study the Bible much before my cancer, I felt *propelled* towards it after my up-close and personal encounter with the Living God. After that life changing experience, I had a deep unquenchable thirst to know more about Jesus, so I met Him in Scripture. People may wonder why I'm such a cheerleader for our Lord. With my life experiences, how could I not be? Mitzi once told me, "I wish I had what you have, but without going through all you did to get it." *Ha!* I thought. *Not possible! You have to go* through *the desert to get to the other side.*

A few years after completing radiation at Mary Bird Perkins Cancer Center, I was asked to be the keynote speaker at their leadership banquet honoring their doctors and major donors. It was a struggle for me to allow myself to become vulnerable enough to share my most intimate faith experiences with complete strangers. There is always the risk of embarrassment or ridicule. Determined to keep my promise to God that I would share our story at any given opportunity, I accepted the challenge. Writing the ten minute speech was the easy part. Had I known that there would be 250 people in attendance, I might have re-negotiated my terms with God, but in this situation, ignorance was indeed bliss.

Despite having a panic attack in the women's restroom beforehand, I evidently delivered a pretty good speech. I received a warm thank you note from Mary Bird Perkins saying they had been "inundated with calls and emails filled with glowing compliments on my inspiring presentation" and that I had shared it "with such eloquence and grace." Huh?! Who knew? It's amazing what we can accomplish with God as our teammate.

Chapter Two

Beloved Ancestors

To help you better understand my strong faith which has its origins in family, let me go back a few generations and introduce you to my loved ones. Captain Louis F. Young, my mom's maternal grandfather, was a coastwise veteran master pilot, which means that he was an experienced domestic sea captain sailing around the Eastern Seaboard. Born in 1860 in French Canada, Louis grew up in Connecticut, thirty miles from the Atlantic Ocean. As a boy, he loved the sea and always dreamed of captaining his own ship. Everyone told him he was too "young" to become a sailor, so he ran away from home in the eighth grade and changed his name from Louis Ayotte to Louis Young.

Eventually, the winds took Captain Young to Madisonville, Louisiana. There he met a lady named Carmelite Currow and her best friend Maggie Stein. In 1894, Louis and Carmelite were married, but sadly she died about six months later. Louis and Maggie, both missing Carmelite, turned to each other for consolation and two years later married, vowing to name their first daughter Carmelite. That's how my grandmother got her name, Carmelite Alice Young.

Even though he was often at sea, Captain Young stayed very close to his five children – Earl, Joe, Carmelite, Marie, and Gladys. He mailed them a postcard from wherever his ship docked, encouraging them as any good father would. He wrote to my Grandma Carmelite, "Are you helping your mama do the dishes? Papa" when she was only five years old. The postcard was dated 1907. How sweet is that?! To Earl he wrote, "Be a good boy. Papa" To Maggie he wrote, "We are coming slow but sure. With love and kisses to all. Louis." Awww! That's so tender and loving.

Everyone seemed to have saved the postcards that Captain Young wrote so faithfully. He was in Jamestown, Virginia in 1907 for the 300th anniversary of its founding, and judging from the picture on the postcard, it was quite a celebration! Marie got one in 1913 from the "New Grand Central Terminal in New York City." I even have one of the Venerable Sister Thérèse of Lisieux in 1921, four years before she became a saint. To me, the most special thing about these historic postcards is reading the sentiments written by my great-grandfather to my Grandma Carmelite when she was just five years old. I remember when *I* was a young child, sitting at my grandma's knees while she prayed the rosary. I witnessed her and my grandpa pray so often, that the importance of faith in our lives was knitted into the fabric of my being. Captain Young's love for travel also profoundly influenced generations both past and present. I once expressed to my mom how much I loved to travel, and she said, "It's in your blood honey! It's in your blood."

Captain Young, Maggie, and their growing family lived a block away from the Tchefuncte River in Madisonville, Louisiana. He bought the house in 1899 for $400 cash. The promissory note was written on an old envelope and the postmark is 1898. It says $200 down and $200 due in two weeks. I also have, not only his bill of sale purchasing the property, but I also have the previous owner's bill of sale from 1874!

Their house was interestingly shaped, similar to a shotgun house but with bedrooms on either side. Captain Young would call those tiny bedrooms "cabinettes" because they were set up a bit like cabins on a ship of the day. Their house was in the heart of town a block from the river; the riverfront itself was an industrial area for workers who would haul freight on and off the boats. Their house got the cool, crisp breezes, but none of the fracás. In his later years, Captain Young commanded the steamboat Susquehanna, carrying passengers from New Orleans to Mandeville to Madisonville and back.

Maggie Young, in addition to raising five children, was very dedicated to civic improvement and educational progress. She worked tirelessly at her church and did many charitable deeds.

Following an illness of several months, Maggie died in 1929 at the young age of fifty-three.

Captain Young served his country in WWI as a Lieutenant in the Navy. After the Great War, he was an active member of the American Legion and Woodmen of the World. My mom, Jeanne, was particularly close to the Captain and loved him dearly. She was only ten years old when he passed away in 1937, but her memories of him remained vivid throughout her life and she passed them down to me.

Both Earl and Joe followed in their father's footsteps becoming sea captains. Uncle Earl served as a Lieutenant Commander in the Merchant Marines during World War II, and then went on to be an international sea captain who brought back many exotic finds from the Orient. My family still treasures the special memento of the America flag that wrapped Uncle Earl's coffin for his military funeral. It has only forty-eight stars on it.

Carmelite and her sister Marie, whom we called "Ree," slept together in the same antique bed that my mother, my daughter, and I all slept in while growing up. Soon it will be passed on to my granddaughter, Elizabeth, making it five generations in one bed!

I have an article that appeared in the society column of the local newspaper, *The St. Tammany Farmer*, in 1907 describing Grandma's fifth birthday. It is as follows:

> Little Miss Carmelite Young entertained a large number of her young friends at the residence of her parents, Captain and Mrs. Young, last Sunday evening. The occasion was the fifth anniversary of her birthday and a good time was had by all. The little folks were entertained by games, and singing, and jumping of the rope. A large table was placed under the pecan trees and was tastefully decorated with white flowers. Those present were...

It went on to list 30+ guests, some of whom I knew. What fun!

Grandma Carmelite was a strikingly beautiful woman. She had jet black hair and dark brown eyes. I'm sure many a man gazed into her chestnut eyes and saw Evangeline, the heroine from Longfellow's novel popular in the early 1900s. An invitation to a welcome home dance after World War I at the historic Southern Hotel in Covington and a completely full dance card are a testament to Carmelite's popularity. There were twenty different men that signed up to dance with her that night.

One of Grandma Carmelite's first jobs was playing the piano at the picture show in Madisonville for the silent movies. There was always a piano playing in the background to heighten or lower the suspense of the film. That always struck me as an extremely interesting job.

Another interesting tidbit of information is that Carmelite's wedding memory book describes the first time she laid eyes on Grandpa Leo; she was almost seventeen and Leo was a dapper young gent of twenty-one.

> "On Sunday May 18, 1919, a boy came along in a car and stopped and talked to Ida. She introduced me to him. He was a boy from Covington and his name was Leo LeBlanc. I had heard so much about him that I decided to take a good look at him and see what I thought of him. We went to the May festival in Covington with him and so I had all the afternoon to look at him, but every time I would look at him, he was looking at me, but I finally decided that he was one of the nicest boys I had ever met, and although that day seems so far away, I have never changed my opinion of him and know I never will."

Awww! So sweet!

My Grandpa Leo's family was one of the original French Acadian families who moved to the wilderness of Canada in the

22

1600s. They settled in Acadié, now known as Nova Scotia. When the French were expelled from Canada in the mid 1700s, Leo's family migrated South and settled near Houma, Louisiana. Fast forward 200 years and my grandpa was born thirty minutes south of Houma in Montegut, Louisiana, a small fishing village not far from the Gulf of Mexico.

Leo's father was Elmá LeBlanc and his mother Eldá. Elmá and Eldá moved their family to Covington and opened a grocery store, LeBlanc's Grocery and Meat Market. Before he got married, Leo worked at the grocery store with his father. However, Grandpa was an industrious man and a tireless worker and he knew that someday he would spread his wings and start a business of his own.

Leo owned a Model T and would often drive the seven miles from Covington to Madisonville to court Carmelite. Four years after they met, Leo proposed to Carmelite and their engagement announcement appeared in the local newspaper, *The St. Tammany Farmer,* as follows:

Engagement of Miss Young Announced

Capt. and Mrs. L.F. Young announce the engagement of their eldest daughter, Carmelite Alice, to Mr. Leo LeBlanc, the wedding to take place in the early spring. Miss Young, a Madisonville lassie, is pretty, accomplished, and very popular with the younger circles. She is at present employed in discharging the duties of assistant cashier at the Madisonville Branch of the Covington Bank & Trust Co. Mr. LeBlanc is the eldest son of Mr. and Mrs. E.E. LeBlanc, of Covington, and is manager of the Grapico Bottling Works there, being numbered among the community's most prominent and well-liked young men.

When Leo and Carmelite married in 1924, Calvin Coolidge was president, prohibition was going strong, and America was in the midst of the Roaring Twenties. The following is a snippet of their wedding announcement which appeared in the newspaper:

LeBlanc – Young

A wedding of interest during the past week was that of Miss Carmelite Young, daughter of Captain and Mrs. L.F. Young, of Madisonville, to Mr. Leo Joseph LeBlanc, son of Mr. and Mrs. E.E. LeBlanc, of Covington. The wedding was celebrated Wednesday, July 23, at nine o'clock nuptial Mass in St. Catherine's Catholic Church, Madisonville, Rev. Father Athmar Bliel officiating.

The church was beautifully decorated for the occasion, the entire effect with the light summery costumes of the bridal party, which were especially pretty, made a very lovely picture....

The bride was given away by her father and wore a gown of white georgette trimmed in lace and ribbon. Her veil of illusion was bound with orange blossoms and she carried a bouquet of bride's roses and lilies of the valley. The attendants wore dresses of georgette and lace, Miss Gladys Young wearing light green, Miss Policar lavender and Miss Milloit pink. All wore hats to match and carried bouquets of roses....

An informal reception followed the ceremony at the bride's home. In cutting the wedding cake the ring fell to Mr. Lawrence Frederick, the button to Mr. Allen LeBlanc, and the wish-bone to Mr. Earl LeBlanc. Later in the day Mr. and Mrs. LeBlanc left by motor for a trip to the Gulf Coast.

The traditional southern wedding pulls mentioned in the previous paragraph were silver charms hidden in the wedding cake. They were festive ways to symbolize who will be the next to get married (ring), who will have children soon (button) and who will have a wish come true (wish-bone.)

Leo and Carmelite lived in the middle of Covington in a small house that they expanded over the years. Leo built the garage and workshop himself. A few years ago when an image of the house flashed across the television screen in a commercial promoting Louisiana, my heart leapt in my throat with sentiment and joy. There was nothing but love sown there.

In 1930, six years after Leo married Carmelite, he owned LeBlanc Bottling Works. The soda bottles created for his business are now collector's items and the few we have are treasured family heirlooms.

Grandpa Leo, a carpenter at heart, crafted beautiful wooden items for his family. During the Depression, he made my Grandma Carmelite a lovely card table from small scraps of wood two or three inches long, which was all he had to work with at the time. In the corners of the table, he painted a club, a heart, a diamond, and a spade. It's simply breathtaking and completely unique – priceless because it was made with a great deal of love and hard work. LeBlanc is stamped on the back of the table like an artist's signature on a painting.

Throughout his life, Leo made tables, benches, and bookcases for his home and those of his two daughters, Jeanne and Margaret. A treasure of mine is a little duck clothespin holder that he made for my mama. I use it every day to hold my notes, bills and other important items so I won't lose them. Grandpa also built a cupboard for his kitchen to hold groceries; my family used that same cupboard as a "homework cabinet." Grandpa and Grandma used the three shelves to store their canned goods; my children, their great-grandchildren, used it to store school papers. It may not be fancy, but it's sturdy and I love it!

Despite the fact that Leo only had a sixth grade education, he did quite well for himself. He worked hard all of his life and learned the invaluable lesson that a penny saved is a penny earned. He discovered that there is no force on earth more powerful than compound interest. Living beneath your means is a vastly underrated survival skill; I highly recommend it for anyone wishing to retire.

Carmelite was 5'2" and Leo was 6 feet tall. He used to say that he could "eat soup off her head." When they got married, Carmelite was pretty petite, but by the time I knew her, she was rather rotund. Grandma remained just as beautiful as she aged, keeping her long, black hair pinned in braids across her head like Heidi, the heroine in my favorite childhood book. I loved them both SO MUCH! I remember them both praying the rosary every day and watching *Gunsmoke* on Monday nights and *Lawrence Welk* on Sundays. Carmelite inherited her father's love of travel. My grandparents' home movies show them at the Grand Canyon, the Smoky Mountains and other national landmarks. Grandma died when I was in the eighth grade.

Grandpa Leo always kept us laughing. He was full of fun, full of life, full of joy. Endlessly patient, Grandpa loved children. With a gleam in his eyes, he would tell us riddles like, "Your Grandma was Young until I married her."

We would say, "Did she get old once you married her, Grandpa?"

He'd answer, "No, but she was Young until I married her."

When our family ate Sunday dinner with our grandparents, and my brother or I would ask Grandpa to pass the salad, he would joke, "I can't say salad. I can only say saladé."

We would exclaim, "But Grandpa! You just said it!"

He would chuckle and reply, "No. No. I can't say salad, I can only say saladé."

We would laugh and laugh. As children, we thought that was so funny. When I started researching my genealogy, I was surprised to learn that French was Grandpa Leo's first language, as he had never mentioned it. Now the saladé joke makes much more sense.

Grandpa Leo would play cards to pass the time. When contemplating his next move in solitaire, he'd say, "'Let's see! Let's see!,' said the blind man." Once a week he and his friends would have a poker game.

If he was sick, we'd inquire how he was feeling. He'd always say, "No use to complain" – and he never did. Grandpa often quoted a man he knew, who told him, "Ya pays ya money, ya takes ya choice." Truer words were never spoken.

Leo was a wonderful man, very kind, loving, and gentle. In the twenty-four years I knew him, I never heard him raise his voice. To this day, it warms my heart to think of him. He was honest to the core; his word was his bond. Grandpa was very civic-minded, serving on the Covington City Council for twenty-four years. Greatly loved by all – black and white, male and female, young and old – his appeal was universal.

After Grandpa died, Mom urged me to keep his memory alive. Here's to you, Mom! Leo J. Leblanc, and everything he stood for, lives on.

Chapter Three

Jeanne's Upbringing

Mom told me that when she was growing up during the Depression, her family had to be terribly thrifty in order to survive. During the war years, they would wash their aluminum foil and reuse it again and again because aluminum was in such short supply. They had twelve Christmas ornaments which they would spread out far and wide in order to cover their entire tree. I still have those fragile little gems.

When Jeanne was in high school she did everything and did it well. She was president of her class for four years, maid in the football court, editor of the school newspaper, valedictorian, and maid of honor in the Spring festival – just to name a few. She was even in the band! Whew!

The following newspaper article was written by my fifteen year old mother about her family during WWII. The "young girl" is my mom, Jeanne. "Gran" is her Great-Grandmother, Frances Canulette, Maggie's mother. This story is not only a window into my family history, but it also describes experiences of women in wartime.

Christmas Today and Yesterday

Although this house is not beautiful, as a home it was surely in a class of its own. As the cold wintry wind blows up from the river, grasping every visible thing in its icy hands, it blows gently around this one old house. As if by instinct, the mighty wind seems to relent. Well it should, for it was almost a century ago that it first held conversation in the eaves of this old house. Let us watch for a little while with the wind, and see what goes on here.

As we pause in the yard, a young girl opens the gate and hurries up the steps. She quietly enters the front door. Now we shall have to look in from the window. In the front room, we see a little old lady with lovely gray hair sitting in front of a huge fireplace. The young girl enters with many presents, for this is Christmas Eve.

"Merry Christmas, Gran", she calls. Gran smiles at this happy young lassie, for just looking at her brings back many fond memories.

"Sit down my dear", she gently says, and continues speaking. "The sight of you reminds me of that Christmas when I was just your age, fifteen. There was a war on then, too – the Civil War." "Gosh Gran, I hadn't realized that", replied the young lady. "Tell me, was it so different from now?" Saying this, she pulls her chair up just a wee bit closer as if she dares not miss a single word of these priceless memories.

"Well, it was the third year of the war. By that time most of my schooling had been altogether cut out. The struggle was beginning to reach a climax, but just as today, the coming of the Christ Child brought as a gift, peace and joy to our souls. It was impossible to buy toys and dolls for children; they had to be made at home. My little sister, who was only seven years old, wanted a doll very badly; so my mother made her one".

"But Gran", cries the modern young lady sitting next to her, "how did she do that?"

"Simple enough", replies the little old lady, "She stuffed old clothes with sawdust, and did her best at painting a face on it. The boys' gifts weren't so complicated. They wanted marbles and balls. The marbles were much the same as today, but there were no rubber balls then; no baseballs or footballs either. Like the dolls, they were made at home – out of old stockings rolled tightly together".

For a moment the young girl is speechless. Then she utters a faint,   "Gee-ee". Suddenly, as if just waking from a dream, she jumps up and stands directly in front of the gray haired lady, and exclaims, "Did you have any food, or did you have to go hungry?"

"We had food, but not very much and when we didn't have enough to go around, the men on the Yankee boats in the river would give us food".

At this the girl, who has stood quietly listening, bluntly states that she simply can't believe this. "Why", she replies, "the Yankees were your enemies".

"Yes that is true", said Gran in a low audible tone. "They were our enemies; but my dear, they were Christians, and you must never forget that even in battle they never like to make people, especially women and children, suffer unnecessarily.

At this point of the conversation, we must slip back outside, for someone is coming in the gate. It is now quite dark, but, not too dark to see who enters. My! This time it is not only one young girl, but many people, both young and old. They are all bundled up in over-coats and brightly colored hats and mufflers. They are laughing and singing and carrying many presents that have been brightly wrapped. The wind now makes a lonesome, hollow sound. Yes it is mighty and powerful, but it can well envy this humble little home, a living picture of peace and contentment. Why is this such a happy home? Quick! Let's observe those inside, with the wind, before it moves on. Now the front room is full of people – four generations of one family. They are all proudly showing off the War Bonds, which they've just bought. But what's this? Look over there. Why, there's a sailor, and isn't that a soldier with him? Yes! They're both grandsons of the little old lady with the lovely gray hair! But where is she? Oh! There she is, still in her chair by the fire. Although she doesn't say much, her glistening eyes and her bright smile tell everything. She has seen ninety-two years of joy and sorrow, and this is one of the happiest days of her life. Everyone in the room, from the middle aged man by the fire, Gran's son, to the girl of fifteen, is determined that although they may never all get together again Gran, who has lived so long, shall see the day when once more peace and happiness shall reign the whole world over.

34

Hark! Outside the wind is moving on, but we needn't go. Won't you come inside with me and let me tell you more? What right have I to ask you in and tell you of the loved ones and joys of this family? None other than the fact that I am that happy young girl of fifteen, and the little old lady with the lovely gray hair is not my grandmother, but my great-grandmother.

Jeanne LeBlanc, '44

When reading this article, I didn't realize that my mom had written it until I got to the very end. I was stunned that she was so talented at such a young age. It has the style and tone of a professional writer. I couldn't be more proud of my mom!!

Jeanne graduated from Southeastern Louisiana University in Hammond with a degree in education. Back in the 1940s, the most common profession for women was either teaching or nursing, so my mom became a school teacher. During the summers, she was a camp counselor at an all-girls summer camp in Lake Charles. She stayed at the home of Bea Gordon, a family friend, who owned Gordon's drugstore in Lake Charles. That may seem like an inconsequential tidbit of information, but it was in fact quite serendipitous.

Chapter Four
Stanley's Upbringing

My Dad, Stanley, is quite a character – but first, some background. His mother, Mamie Gariepy, was one of ten children from a large family in Michigan. Mamie was engaged to a man in an arranged marriage, but she didn't like him at all. He threatened to kill her if she left him, but thankfully that didn't stop Mamie from walking away. Wise choice. She hid in her bedroom at home for three months until, in the middle of a cold winter's night in 1913, her father took the bells off his horse and sleigh and drove her to the train station. The train took her to New Orleans, where she lived with relatives while she got back on her feet. In 1919, my grandmother became one of the first registered nurses in the state of Louisiana.

After that, Mamie lived in a boarding house where her future husband, Alton, also resided. At the time, Mamie had a boyfriend. One evening he called her on the house phone and, not wishing to talk to him, she whispered to Alton, "Tell him I'm not here." Alton forcefully replied, "I'm not gonna lie for you! You tell your own damn lies!" And he didn't. *I am so impressed with that!* Mamie apparently was as well because she eventually married Alton.

Dad's father, Alton Bridges, moved with his new bride to McComb, Mississippi where his family owned land. It was during those years that their three sons were born: Alton Jr., Bill, and the little caboose Stanley, all two years apart. Alton farmed for several years but was unable to make a living at it, so he moved his family to New Orleans and began working for the railroad.

Alton worked as a special officer or patrolman for the Illinois Central. He carried a pistol (and a big stick) to keep out the hobos who were trying to hitchhike or steal from the railroad. Yikes! Alton was a tough man. Daddy says he wasn't very big – only 5'9" – but he was thin and wiry and hard as nails. Dad also remembers his father as an intellectual man who would quote line after line of Robert Burns poetry. Dad told me that Alton made only $60 a month, but they always managed to scrape up the $3 a month it cost to send their boys to Catholic schools. That made a powerful impression on me.

In 1930, when Alton Jr. was eleven years old, he stepped on a rusty nail and got lockjaw. The family was eating dinner one night when Junior's jaw muscles locked, and he couldn't close his mouth or swallow. They took him to the hospital, but at that point, there was nothing that could be done. My dad was only seven years old when he kissed his brother for the last time and waved

38

goodbye as he left the room that evening. Alton Bridges Jr. died a painful death a short while after that.

His mother never forgave herself. Being a nurse, Mamie thought she had cleaned the wound thoroughly and didn't take him to get a tetanus shot, which were rarely given back then. Tetanus shots had just been developed in 1924 and didn't become widely available in the United States until the 1940s. Mamie blamed herself for Junior's death for the rest of her life. Alton Jr. had been the apple of her eye and suddenly he was gone. After Bill and Stanley were grown, Mamie and Alton adopted a little girl named Barbara. They'd always wanted a daughter.

Uncle Bill was rough and tough, and loved to fight. When I was a little girl, Dad would tell me that Uncle Bill used to beat him up every day. I asked him, "Dad, how long did Uncle Bill beat you up?" Daddy said proudly, "Until I got bigger than him and beat *him* up."

Dad's family grew up during the tough times of the Great Depression. When Dad and Uncle Bill were ten and twelve, they would sell newspapers on the corner to help the family make ends meet, sometimes earning as much as seventy-eight cents a day!

Seventy-five cents went to help support the family, but their mom let them keep the three cents for candy. Dad was thrilled because, "for a nickel, they could buy a Mr. Goodbar as big as your palm!" The brothers would often encounter bullies on the way home who would try to steal their money. Bill would lag behind and fight them, while Dad ran home with the money. The poignancy of that story never fails to tug on my heartstrings. They were just children!

In school, Uncle Bill was not a very good student and failed a couple of grades. He was most likely dyslexic, but it was not diagnosed then. Of course, it didn't help that they had to change schools every two years because of transfers in Alton's job. My dad caught up with Bill in the fifth grade. After that, they were in the same grade even though there was a two year age difference.

Dad told me that one night at bath time, there was such a ruckus in the bathroom his mom thought the roof was going to cave in. When she walked in there, Dad and Uncle Bill were fist fighting buck naked over who was going to get in the bathtub first! You see, they could only afford one hot bath for the boys, so they fought over who would get in first with the clean, hot water.

Back in Mississippi when they were twelve and fourteen, Stanley and Bill would skip school to go swimming in the creek. When they came home, their eyes were red, their skin was filthy, and they were sunburned all over. Their mom asked knowingly,

"How was school today?" The truant boys replied, "Oh it was good! It was really good." Boy! Mamie tore into them because she knew they had skipped school. Their mama never let them get away with shenanigans like that.

Dad told me another very interesting story. He said that his neighbors were sharecroppers, and one day, they paid him and his brother Bill to help them pick cotton. They were teenagers at the time, and Dad said he knew they hadn't done a very good job. Stanley and Bill came home from their sweaty, back-breaking work and got washed up to go to the picture show.

Having already heard complaints from the neighbors about the cotton episode, Alton got home and picked up a poker by the fireplace and gave both sons a whack. He asserted, "Boys! If you take someone's money to do a job, *you do it, and do it well, or you are stealing.*" There was no picture show for those two that night!

Alton made them go back right then and there to finish the job and apologize to the neighbors. Finishing the job left them with the enduring memory of a job well done; the apology ensured that they took ownership of their wrong doing and reconciled with their neighbors. Moved by the lessons he learned that day, Daddy worked extremely hard all of his life to provide for our family. Dad is now ninety-five years old and enjoying his 30th year in retirement. *Hard lessons bear fruit.*

Since he had failed two grades, nineteen year old Bill was drafted for World War II before he graduated from high school. The draft notice came the summer prior to his senior year. Bill had been kicked out of a lot of schools for fighting, and my grandmother knew that if her son went off to war without a high school degree, he would never make it to college.

Bill only had four months before he had to report for active duty, so Mamie paid a visit to the nuns at an all-girls school nearby, St. Mary of the Pines. She asked them if they would tutor her son and help him graduate; with a degree, he would be able to go directly into college after he came home. The Sisters agreed.

Dad bragged gleefully about his big brother, saying "We all went to Bill's high school graduation. He was the valedictorian and the only student! The band played, the cheerleaders cheered. It was just like a regular graduation, but there was only one student."

Mamie was wise to have her son complete his high school education before going overseas. Bill served our country for five years in World War II and when he got home, he went straight into college on the G.I. Bill. He graduated with a degree in Journalism and worked for a newspaper until he retired.

In Mississippi in the 1930s, high school only went to the eleventh grade. After Dad graduated from high school, he and several friends worked in California for a couple of years as riveters for North American Aviation. Building airplanes in the war effort, they made B-25 bombers and B-51 mustang fighters. Dad reported that he was "living in high cotton in Hollywood!" For the first time in his life, he had some spending money.

The big bands would hit Los Angeles a day early to play a weekend engagement at a nightclub like the Orpheum Theater. Every Thursday night, for the price of a movie ticket at the neighboring theater, Dad got to see both a movie and a free show. He remembers dancing to hits like "Smoke Gets in Your Eyes" from Artie Shaw, and "Rhapsody in Blue" from Paul Whiteman.

In Hollywood, when a movie was being filmed at night, they would shine the klieg lights and you could drive by and watch. Dad once saw Claudette Colbert filming at a train station. When Dad played golf, he saw Bob Hope, William Frawley, and other celebrities on the course. Hearing these stories from my dad developed my love of movies as a child.

Stanley registered for the draft in California and at ninety-five years of age, he still remembers his draft number. Mind like a steel trap! Sent to Keesler Army Airfield in Mississippi, Dad trained for eight months before being shipped out to Foggia, Italy to serve with the 15th Air Force Division of the U.S. Army. He spent Christmas, New Year's, and his twenty-first birthday on a ship headed to war. After zigzagging the whole way to keep from being torpedoed, the convoy of 450 vessels reached Italy 26 days later. Dad prayed the entire way.

In the war, Dad was a cook. He used to refer to himself as the "Chief Cook and Bottle Washer" because that's exactly what he did. Because of his lack of a college education, the only opportunities for him in the Army were either to be a truck driver or a cook. Dad figured he was less likely to be shot at as a cook, so that's what he volunteered for. That's my Dad! Always thinking on his feet!

During that time, Dad befriended a young Italian man named Luigi Giacomello, an Italian national a bit younger than himself who was caught up in the war in Europe. The Italian people in that area were poverty stricken. Luigi for instance, didn't have much to eat, so my dad would sneak him food from the kitchen.

One time Dad put Luigi in an American soldier uniform in order to sneak him into a big USO show. Those were the shows hosted by Bob Hope with Hollywood stars and beautiful girls that would entertain the troops. Dad snuck Luigi in and told him "Keepá, you mouth, shut!" Not knowing each other's language they somehow communicated as people tend to do. Dad didn't want Luigi to speak because that would be a dead give-away that he wasn't an American soldier. If he had been caught, Dad could have been court-martialed. Yikes!

Mom and Dad's first trip to Europe was in 1973 to Italy. There was a bartender at the hotel bar whose last name was Giacomello; Dad enlisted his help in tracking down Luigi. Apparently that was harder than it seems because in that region of Italy, Giacomello was as common as Smith or Jones. There were forty Giacomellos in the phone book in Luigi's home town. After several false starts, the bartender finally spoke to a relative of Luigi's who said that Luigi was living in Québec, Canada. Finally, Dad got the prized phone number.

There was so much excitement in our home the night that Daddy called Luigi and re-connected. We all gathered around the phone, listening to every word. Dad and Luigi didn't miss a beat in their friendship, picking up right where they had left off thirty years earlier. The love shared and bonds created during that frightful and traumatic time seemed to have only strengthened over the years. The war buddies then spoke every few months.

The following year, Daddy won a Lincoln Continental from a raffle ticket. Dad decided to break it in by driving our family up to Québec to visit Luigi and his wife Lena. Our family stayed in their home for three nights. Luigi owned a five-star restaurant, at the time, the only five-star restaurant in Québec. Every night, Luigi invited our whole family for dinner at his restaurant and wouldn't let us pay a dime. Luigi said, "Your Dad gave me food throughout the war; he probably saved my life! Now it's my turn to feed him." That story still brings tears to my eyes.

Dad's second year in the war, he and a couple of other G.I.'s went on a weekend leave of absence. Since they were serving their country in Italy, they decided to go to the beach on the Adriatic coast. During their journey to the Adriatic Sea, they came across the monastery in San Giovanni Rotondo where Padre Pio lived, now Saint Padre Pio. My dad and his friends went into the monastery and met Padre Pio. Daddy said that he wore brown clothes and had on purple gloves with the fingers cut out to cover his stigmata. Daddy often joked that he should have gone to confession with Padre Pio, known for his great confessions, but that he would still be in there today! Ole Dad – always the jokester!

After his service in the war, Stanley came home and attended pharmacy school at Loyola University New Orleans on the G.I. Bill. Loyola fast-tracked the veterans, who were so much older than the young freshmen, and my dad had his bachelor's degree in pharmacy in three years. I asked Dad what he thought he would have done for a living without the G.I. Bill, since his parents couldn't afford to send him to college, and he replied, "A ditch

digger?" My eyes widened as he continued. "I don't know...
manual labor?? I wasn't qualified for anything else – maybe
stocking shelves in a grocery store?" Wow! Two years of service
in the Army earned my father a college degree which changed his
entire future – financial and otherwise.

Stanley's first job was in Monroe, Louisiana working for
his uncle, Dr. William Bendel. Now, even though he was grateful
to Uncle William for getting him a job, Dad was miserable. He told
me that Uncle William would come in to the drugstore after
making house calls and throw a stack of thirty to forty
prescriptions down for Dad to fill. Of course, they also had the
normal walk-in business as well. At the end of the day, Uncle
William would call in thirty or forty more prescriptions to be filled
and have delivered. Eventually, my Dad decided to quit that job
but he was too embarrassed to face Uncle William and tell him he
was leaving. Instead, he took off one night after work and headed
for a job interview with Gordon's Drugstore in Lake Charles.

Stanley drove to Lake Charles at night, leaving Monroe
after working all day. He fell asleep at the wheel and hit a tree,
totaling his car. Miraculously unharmed, Dad climbed out of the
vehicle, and hitchhiked his way to Lake Charles. The next morning
he got the job, started working right away, and never looked back.
I tell you, we Bridges are made from sturdy stock.

Chapter Five
The Love Story

To re-cap from the previous chapter, my dad got the job at
Gordon's Drugstore in Lake Charles, and my mom was living with
the pharmacist and owner Bernice Gordon in her house over the
drugstore. Mom told me that one day, she went into Gordon's to
make a purchase and wrote a check for it. Dad was waiting on her
at the cash register. He took her check, studied it, and then said
"I'll need your phone number, Miss." My mom's eyes twinkled as
she told me, "He *knew* I was living with the owner of the drug
store, so he *knew* where I lived." Stanley called Jeanne for a date,
and the rest is history.

Mom and Dad got married in her hometown of Covington
at St. Peters Catholic Church. Fortunately for them, there was an
opening for a pharmacist at O.J. Hebert's Drugs at the corner of
Boston and New Hampshire streets in Covington. "Uncle Oliver,"
as we called him, was nearly seventy years old and was looking for
a young protégé to eventually take over his business. It was a
match made in heaven. Oliver Hebert treated my dad like the son
he never had. Nine months later, Uncle Oliver had a heart attack,
after which he sold the drugstore to my dad.

Hebert Drugs was the type of soda fountain drugstore where everybody knew everybody and no one was a stranger. The following is an excerpt from an article which appeared in the New Orleans newspaper, *The Times-Picayune* about the small town of Covington.

> In 1939, a customer brought a live chicken to the drugstore asking Mr. Hebert to keep it for her while she shopped. He carried the wriggling chicken to the yard behind the store and when she returned in a taxi, he couldn't find the chicken. He told her that he was too busy to retrieve it then, but he'd deliver it to her house on his way home. He called his wife, Cecile, and asked. "Do we have a chicken?" There were two chickens cooked for dinner, she said. Mr. Hebert delivered one to the customer. Another example of the warm, hometown vibe of Covington was in 1937, a stranger from the city came to town without a tie and was invited to dine out. Would Mr. Hebert please lend him the tie he was wearing? The druggist took the man to his nearby home to select a tie from his wardrobe.

It was into these pleasant environs that my dad arrived and thrived.

My mother, Jeanne, taught high school English at Covington High School for six years until my brother Lou was born. Then she stayed home to be a full time mother. Mom and Dad had a very hard time having children. Mom had six miscarriages and lost a total of seven babies – one of her pregnancies was twins – before they eventually had my brother, Lou. Happy Birthday indeed!

After Mom had Lou, the doctor warned her not to get pregnant again because it might jeopardize her life. Having an incredibly strong faith, Mom prayed to the Virgin Mary our Mother, and to St. Ann, Mary's mother, asking for their intercession. "If I have a little girl," she pleaded, "I will name her Mary Ann, and for the rest of her life I will call her by both names in your honor." Well, along came a bouncing baby girl and even though Ann is my middle name, I've always gone by both.

Two years after I was born, Mom had another baby. Apparently Jeanne had been exposed to German Measles while she was pregnant, and Bonnie Mary was extremely deformed at birth, living only fourteen minutes. The doctor baptized Bonnie Mary before she died. Mom never saw her. Years later, my anguished mother described the devastation of going to the hospital expecting to bring home a baby, and leaving without one.

Stanley and Jeanne were charter members of the mutual admiration society. They respected each other immensely and had a beautiful relationship built on love, trust, and a shared faith.

Mom always greeted Daddy at the door, telling me, "Dad works hard all day to support us. The least I can do is get up to greet him at the door."

Mom cooked a delicious, hot, nutritionally balanced meal every night. Dad worked from 8am to 7pm five days a week and from 8am to noon on Wednesdays and Sundays. We ate supper about 7:15 each night, as soon as Daddy got home. Our family prayed before every meal, thanking God for our food. In our home there was always a peaceful, loving, calmness brought upon by my mother's gentle demeanor and gracious manner. Jeanne was a true lady in every sense of the word. She was refined, articulate, intelligent, and courteous at all times.

Chapter Six

Growing Up

My brother, Lou, was always very old for his age. Mama told me that as a child, Lou used to read the dictionary at night to learn more words. That was mind boggling to an ordinary kid like me. I remember one day when Lou was sick, his slippers were on the floor all neat and tidy. Apparently, I accidently knocked one of them askew (or maybe on purpose) and Lou told Mama on me. He said "Mama! Mary Ann's messing up my slippers!" Haha! We were a fine pair!

My earliest memories as a child are of feeling very safe and very loved. Over my bed hung two pictures: the famous English painting, *The Blue Boy,* and next to it was a beautiful ballerina in arabesque. Gazing daily on those pieces blossomed in me a deep love of the arts. Mom told me years later that they were the tops of cookie cans she had just hung on the wall.

Every night after Mom and I knelt to say our prayers, I'd scramble into bed, relishing the warm and comfortable feeling it provided. Mom would pull up the crisp white sheet and "tuck me in to my chinny-chin-chin." She then kissed me on my cheek and told me, "I love you." Turning off my lamp, Mom would whisper,

"Sweet dreams" before she tiptoed out of my room. Our nightly routine rarely varied. It gave me a great deal of comfort and security.

Every morning during the school year, Mom would cook a hot, delicious breakfast. After saying Grace and The Morning Offering, which dedicated our day to Christ, we ate together as a family. Our routine went like clockwork, probably because Dad had served in the Army and he liked it that way.

Having older parents had a profound effect on my life. When I was born, Mom was thirty-three and Dad was thirty-eight and they liked things quiet and orderly. While friends around me lived lives that seemed fun and playful, my life was very structured and intellectual.

When I was about five years old, I was at my dad's drugstore standing in front of the big candy display. I recall looking at the M&Ms, salivating. I vividly remember thinking, *well, my dad owns this drugstore, so he owns everything in it, therefore we own those M&Ms so it's okay for me to eat them.* In that way my little child-like mind rationalized theft.

So I took a pack of M&Ms in my grubby little hands and snuck outside. I was standing on the sidewalk eating them when my mom came out and saw me. Oh Lord! Mama went back inside the store and told my dad who promptly left the pharmacy, took me home, and spanked my little butt. I learned a valuable lesson that day. The spanking may have stung briefly, but the lesson Dad taught me – how wrong it is to steal – lasted a lifetime. *Thank God for strong fathers.*

Mama loved dreary days in the dead of winter because it gave her the opportunity to curl up in bed and read a good book. One day when I was four or five, I remember it raining outside, and Mama put us in Lou's bed and read aloud to us. Using different voices for every character, Mom made the story come alive. She would draw us into a world quite unlike our own. Simply by using our imagination, we traveled to far off places, visualizing scenery painted with the authors' words. That is how we developed our life-long love of reading – our mother read aloud to us.

As soon as we could write our names, we got our very own library card and checked out as many books as we possibly could. Mom, Lou, and I were voracious readers; Dad may have been one as well, but he worked over sixty hours a week to provide for our family, and when he got home he was tired.

Lou and I rarely fought. I think we genuinely liked each other – either that, or the fact that fighting wasn't allowed in the house. It was against the rules – at least, that's what my mom told me…hmmm. During the summer we played board games, our favorites being Chess, Chinese checkers, and Risk: The Game of Global Domination. Each one taught strategy and planning ahead, valuable life skills.

My happiest memories as a child were our vacations. When we left our driveway we left the world behind. There were exciting new places, the rules were relaxed – why, we could even eat in the car! Can you imagine?! It was the highlight of my year. Our family was so carefree, and I just cherished that. We never went anywhere fancy. Biloxi was our getaway until I was eight, ironic because Mom couldn't swim and hated sand. Back in the day, Biloxi was the Destin of its time, yet we never stepped foot on the beach.

The Sea Gull Motel, a small, picturesque motor hotel, welcomed us warmly every year. With homey cabins on either side of a long straight road, cars could pull up directly in front of their room – a plus for my dad. The pink azaleas always seemed to be in bloom.

Mass at St. Michael's Church was something we looked forward to every year, as it had a sea shell as its roof and thirty-six stained glass windows forming the circular shape of the building.

After mass each year, our family would walk around and talk about the saints pictured in the stain glass windows. To this day, I enjoy learning about the lives of the saints!

Back at the motel, Daddy would take us swimming since Mom's fair skin sunburned so easily. I remember Dad wearing this boxer length, purple and white, paisley print swimsuit when we went swimming (I kid you not!) Basically, we would just play in the pool. At the time we thought it was such a great big pool; however, when we went back as adults to visit, I realized it was about the size of a shoe box.

I still remember our time there so fondly. We slept late, ate sandwiches for lunch, swam in the afternoon, and played shuffleboard every evening. Supper might be home-made spaghetti or chili. Sunday, after we checked out, we ate breakfast at the restaurant next door, the Friendship House. That was our big splurge for the week and gosh was that exciting! Waffles for breakfast – Yumm!

Eight Flags over Mississippi, a quaint amusement park in Biloxi, was our outdoor adventure. A train circled its perimeter and there was a deer park where we could feed the deer; our favorite, however, was the Wild West cowboy show. It had a huge set – maybe a city block long. The bad guys, known by their black hats, rode into town to rob the bank. The townspeople, shocked that men could be so brazen, had their hands in the air, trembling.

But never fear – the sheriff appears!! Tall, handsome, and wearing a white hat, he burst onto the scene to save the day. The drama always ended with a shoot out. Somehow, the sheriff managed to kill all the bank robbers and their lookouts who were hiding on the tops of different buildings. Golly! He sure was a good shot!

Luckily for us, the Wild West had a saloon and dance hall where we could go into the air conditioning and wet our whistle. Lou and I would belly up to the bar and order a sarsaparilla, basically an old-timey root beer. The beautiful dancing girls did the Can-Can, the "new" dance from Paris. The dancers were all pretty and had great figures; they were easy on the eyes as my dad would say. We had so much fun! Did I mention that the sarsaparilla came in a big ole frosty mug?! My parents were way too thrifty to buy soft drinks at home, so we only got them the few times a year we ate out. Soft drinks were a big deal to a kid in the 1960s – at least to this kid it was!

Our first "real" vacation was to the Smoky Mountains when I was nine. Anticipation built as we saw barn after barn urging us to SEE ROCK CITY! *What on earth was Rock City?* I wondered. I still remember the thrill of seeing the mountains for the first time! We saw seven states from the top of Lookout Mountain and were in awe of Rock City. We barely made it through Fat Man's Squeeze and we lived to tell all about the rickety-old, swinging bridge. Gazing at the stunning views from Lover's Leap, I never could have imagined such beauty existed!

After that vacation, we mostly went to places like Six Flags, Astroworld, and Disney World. Our family went to Disney World the first summer it was open. Now that was a fun trip! It opened October 1, 1971, and we went the following July. There were only two hotels at the time: the Contemporary Resort and the Polynesian Resort. We stayed at the Contemporary, the "A" shaped hotel with the tram going right through the middle of it. Magic Kingdom was the only park there at the time, but we all had a blast, even Mom and Dad! It truly is a magical place.

Chapter Seven

Family and Values

My entire childhood was spent living in Covington, three blocks from the Catholic Church. Mom and Dad bought the property in 1955 and built the house five years later when I was born. They wanted to pay off that debt before they started accumulating more. You don't hear of that much these days.

Mom's parents, Leo and Carmelite, lived five blocks away so when Lou and I were old enough, we would ride our bikes over to visit with them. I remember riding my bike all over town by myself and feeling very safe doing it. Aunt Margaret, Uncle Cecil and their six kids: Peg, Bud, Jim, Lee, and the twins, Jeff and Jan would come from Baton Rouge once a month for Sunday dinner at "Grandma's house." Poor Grandpa! He didn't get any credit for either the house or the visit!

After a delicious dinner of red beans and rice or spaghetti and saladé (remember, Grandpa can't say salad!), the eight of us kids would pile outside to play games. Cowboys and Indians, King of the Hill, and Kick the Can were our go-tos. Having to make our own entertainment in order to escape boredom fostered creativity, ingenuity, and teamwork. It was either that or being stuck in an endless cycle of "What do you want to do?" "I dunno know. What do you want to do?"

Sometimes on Sunday afternoon following Mass, Grandpa Leo and Grandma Carmelite would take Lou and me down to visit Ree and Nannie. You'll remember that Ree was Carmelite's sister, Marie. Well, Nannie was Carmelite's aunt, Maggie's sister, Anastasia. Maggie may have died young, but her sister lived to a ripe old age – well into her nineties. Ree never married and lived in her childhood home with Nannie, who was widowed. Together, they lived in the house on St. John Street purchased for $400 cash.

As an eight year old, I found our visits incredibly boring because there was nothing for us kids to do while the old folks visited – w e l l l l, there was one thing. Ree and Nannie raised chickens, and Lou and I thought that was hysterical. I mean, who in this day and age keeps poultry in their yard? After all, it's the sixties! Everyone knows you can get chicken and eggs at the grocery store! But anyway, Lou and I would go outside and chase the chickens. Actually, I think *we* liked it a lot more than the *chickens* did. (We gave a whole new meaning to scrambled eggs!) Our "reward" for being so patient was a soft serve ice cream cone from Badeaux's Drive In, which cost all of ten cents. The four of us sat in Grandpa's 1969, green, Buick LeSabre and enjoyed that delicious frozen delight, watching carefully not to let any of it drip down on our fingers.

Just like Grandpa Leo had his sayings, Dad had his own sayings which would always make us laugh. When Mama would cook something especially good for supper, Dad would say, "Ah delizioso! That's Italian for delicious!" (as if we couldn't figure it out). Somehow it was funny every time; probably because it meant that Dad was in a good mood and we loved that. He would also sing "Shave and a haircut, two bits!" around the house. Most people know the beat, but not the lyrics.

My dad's brother, Uncle Bill, lived in Shreveport. He and Aunt Mary had three children; Mary Susan was the oldest, followed by Duncan and then Denise. Denise was about five years older than me. We saw them every other year or so.

In our family, Christmas was always a very big deal. After Grandma died, we would alternate get-togethers at our house one year and Aunt Margaret's the next. My mom planned days ahead of time, making sure every last detail was taken care of by Christmas Eve, so that on the next day, we could relax and enjoy each other. Everything was so nice. The house was spick and span, the table was beautifully set, and the name place cards were attached to little boxes of chocolate candy wrapped festively for the holiday.

In 1970, I turned ten years old. At the drugstore, there was this cool new gadget called a clock radio. I marveled over the fact that the clock and the radio were literally connected into one device! It was electric, but had a battery backup, and the AM/FM radio slid off to become portable. Casey Kasem's American Top 40 to go, please! There was even a snooze switch where you could actually roll over and catch a few more winks. I know!! Hard to believe, right?! But this was the 1970s, and technology was cutting edge.

The price tag was 70 dollars, and I was pretty sure that I didn't have the funds for it. I didn't even need to check my piggy bank. So I did what most young kids would do, I asked my parents for it. Waaah, waaah, waaah, waaaah! That went over like a lead balloon.

"You will have to work for it," Dad said. "You can save up your allowance and do extra chores."

Mom agreed cheerily, "Yes! You can easily earn enough money to buy that clock radio on your own."

What were they thinking?? Never before had I heard crazy talk like that from my parents, but I was raised to honor my father and my mother, and honor them I did. For three long months I worked hard, earning a dollar here, two dollars there, saving every penny until I finally earned the 70 dollars. Money in hand, I rode my bicycle to the drugstore as fast as I could to buy this new wave of electronic gadgetry. Parking my bike out front, I strode into the store proudly and made my way over to the glass showcase where all the really hot items were kept. Shocked, I couldn't believe my eyes! My cherished link to the future of technology was sold! With a broken heart and tears in my eyes, I silently left the store, picked up my bike from the sidewalk and slowly began the long ride home.

Later that evening, after the drugstore closed, Mom and Dad sat me down and presented me with a gift. You guessed it – the clock radio!! My parents wanted to teach me the value of a dollar and the immense satisfaction of working hard for something and earning it. That lesson changed my life. Learning how to save money and gaining control of my spending habits helped me on my journey from a spoiled child into a mature adult with a strong work ethic. I am grateful to Mom and Dad for their foresight and self-discipline. "No" is the biggest character building word in the dictionary.

My elementary school, St. Peter's, was four blocks from my house and, to show you what a small town Covington was, my high school, Saint Scholastica Academy, was *five* blocks from my house. Mom drove Lou and me to and from school every day, so my parents saw no need for us to have a car. I remember being embarrassed as it seemed like everyone else in my class had their own car.

Growing up in a neighborhood full of boys, I was very much a tomboy. I tagged along with Lou and his friends and tried to keep up. They were all two years older than me, so I quickly learned to hold my own and to be tough. That toughness helped me survive cancer. God uses all things.

Like most kids, Lou and I had chores to do, such as emptying the dishwasher and helping clean up after supper. My parents emphasized that anyone who eats on a plate should be able to clean that plate – male or female. We were equal opportunity children.

On Saturdays, we cleaned our bathroom and swept the porches and carport. With the car backed out of the carport, Lou and I seized the opportunity to try out our new roller skates. We would skate around and around in tiny little circles wearing our metal skates with the little key to adjust the size. They were, after all, one size fits all skates!

Our first pets were two goldfish named Butch and Joe, quickly joined by Lightning, a mutt. Our next dog was also a mutt from the pound that we named, believe it or not, Darvon, after the pain reliever. By that time, there were three of us working in the pharmacy and we wanted a unique name. Darvon was the dog about whom our veterinarian once told us, "Y'all must be giving that dog UGLY pills!" The NERVE of that man saying that about our beloved dog! Lou and I could clearly see Darvon was quite beautiful. Hmmph!!

When we were older, we graduated to a purebred, a Schnauzer. ("Watch your language!" Dad would say.) Before our family got the dog, we chose the name Eli Lilly for the drug company that my parents owned stock in. If it was a boy we would call him Eli, and if it was a girl we would call her Lilly. Lilly was a lap dog. In later years, I looked back at pictures of Darvon and compared him to Lilly and *darn* it if that vet wasn't right! Darvon was a strikingly ugly dog. Who knew?

Chapter Eight

Remember When

I have fond memories of growing up in a small southern town in the 1960s. In Covington, life was very simple – Americana at its finest. Covington was the type of town where you baked cookies to welcome a new neighbor and waved a friendly hello at everyone you saw. The mayor, the garbage man, and everyone in between received a wave and a smile to brighten their day.

Times have changed from my childhood to my children's. Back then, we *played* after school, making up games as we went. There were little, if any, organized extracurricular activities. On the other hand, when my children were growing up, they were involved in so many extracurricular activities that it took up a large portion of their time and ours. Organized sports have increased in popularity and importance in a kid's life. We had a lot more down time. People need down time – *even Jesus needed down time!* Matthew 14:23 tells us that after Jesus fed the 5,000, He dismissed the crowd and went off on a mountainside by Himself to pray.

When we were twelve and ten years old, Lou and I would entertain ourselves for *hours* in the summer with only a pair of flip-flops and a porch swing. Creating an elaborate game of catch, we tossed and caught the flip-flop mid-air as we swung. Team names came from cities all over the state like the Covington Catchers and the Franklinton Fliers, as if our game was as important as Major League Baseball. We could even hear the crowd roaring – well actually, we *were* the crowd roaring!

I remember climbing trees. What fun! The heights we attained hidden among the branches seemed to improve our imagination. We were on the mast of a pirate ship (ARRRGH!) or a spy in the army. I haven't seen a kid climb a tree in decades. One of my favorite movies was <u>The Swiss Family Robinson</u>. It was a great story, but I especially loved their tree house.

In 1973 when I was thirteen years old, I began working in my dad's drugstore. I remember 10 cent candy bars going up to 15 cents. Whew! That was a lot of money for us kids! Gas was 35 cents a gallon, stamps were 8 cents, and you could see a movie for a buck fifty. The drugstore was just a mile from our house so I could ride my bike to work. The staff was like family and most everyone in town would come into the store at one point or another. Folks were friendly and always had time for a kind word. Often today, people are in such a rush that sometimes business transactions take place without so much as a greeting exchanged.

One of our best customers was the internationally known author Walker Percy. I remember Dr. Percy being a very soft spoken and humble man. Never asserting his fame for privilege, he would patiently wait in line behind all the customers. Dr. Percy once said, "Covington is a very sleepy little town. The local beer distributor has more name recognition than I do." He wasn't kidding.

Eating out was a rarity for our family. Mom cooked delicious, well-rounded meals and we never felt that we were missing out on anything. I remember when the first "fast food" restaurant came to our area, a Kentucky Fried Chicken in Hammond, a town twenty miles away. We would always stop on our way back home from visiting my grandparents in McComb, Mississippi and get a bucket of chicken. We became friends with the lady who worked there and knew her by name (Miss Judy). We always had a really good conversation whenever we went.

Life was much simpler back then with no big pressure to grow up. I was never offered drugs or knew anyone who did them. Reading was my entertainment! A bookworm as a kid, I devoured all the Nancy Drew books the moment they hit the bookstores. Together, Encyclopedia Brown and I solved the mystery and closed the case. As a youth, I read whodunits and adventure series, like Agatha Christie and Alistair MacLean. In high school, my favorite novel was *Pride and Prejudice* by Jane Austen, with *Anna Karenina* by Leo Tolstoy running a close second. Elizabeth Bennet informed my wit, cautioned me against prejudice, and taught me that there are two sides to every story. From every book I read, a tidbit of wisdom was gleaned. Today I look back and see how great of a role this "supplemental education" had in my life. Many children these days miss out on this opportunity to learn and mature because reading for pleasure comes so low on their priority list. Video games seem to have replaced books in a child's life.

When our parents would go on vacation, Lou and I got to spend the week with Grandpa Leo and Grandma Carmelite. I remember playing endless card games with my Grandpa. A lot of my parents' and grandparents' culture and values were passed down to us simply by the amount of time we spent together over a deck of cards. Conversation flowed easily over a game of battle or bourré.

My grandparents' house seemed hopelessly old-fashioned. The hot water came out of one faucet and the cold out of a second one. There was no central heat, so we slept in an ice cold bedroom with lots of covers, running into the family room as soon as we woke up to warm ourselves by the gas heater. Yet when Grandma and Grandpa built their house in the 1920s, it was state of the art, complete with running water (which many houses did not have), attic fans and space heaters. However, as a child in the modern times of the seventies, I couldn't fully appreciate that.

TV was relatively new when I was young. When I grew up, our favorite shows were *Tarzan, The Brady Bunch*, and *The Partridge Family*, as well as the *Dean Martin Show, Mission Impossible*, and *Mannix*. We especially loved all the Christmas specials. Interestingly enough, we were not allowed to watch *Mary Tyler Moore Show* when we were little. That worked out wonderfully because when I was diagnosed with cancer at thirty-three, I watched all the *Mary Tyler Moore* reruns. Never having seen any of them, they just struck me as incredibly funny. Escapism at its finest!

When Lou and I were growing up, we only had one television in the house, so our family would all watch together. As Dad loved golf that is what often ran on the small, square screen. Dad shot his first hole in one at seventy-six and played golf until he was ninety. Football also received much screen-time in the Bridges' household. I remember when the New Orleans Saints were formed in 1967; my dad was beside himself! Archie Manning was our most memorable quarterback back then (Archie who?), which is why Peyton and Eli grew up in New Orleans. I was a big football fan as a kid; that's when I learned the game. To tell the truth, I think I just enjoyed spending time with my dad. We also watched the Miss America Pageant as a family each year without fail. Dad pulled for Miss Mississippi and we pulled for Miss Louisiana, so there was a healthy rivalry going on in the house.

I have always loved movies. In Covington, going to the theater was an event! When a Disney movie would come to town, Lou and I would look forward to it for weeks in advance. We'd be excited because there were so few movies we could see; our parents only let us see G-rated movies until we were teenagers. (My first R-rated movie was <u>A Star is Born</u>, which burst into theaters when I was fifteen.) I used to keep a notebook of all the movies I had seen, rating them like the movie critic, Gene Shalit, did. My dad always thought that was funny.

Our family went to Mass every Sunday without fail. If we were on vacation, Dad would find a Catholic Church for us to attend. It's what we did. It's what we believed. It's what we stood for. Yes, times have changed – some for the better, some for the worse – but it is always good to remember our roots. Then we can look back and see how far we have come, or how far we have drifted.

Chapter Nine

The High School Years

Saint Scholastica Academy, an all girls, college-prep, Catholic high school located smack dab in the middle of town, was the perfect place for me. Known for their excellent Language Arts program, S.S.A taught me the basic skills I needed to be able to express myself. My Grandma Carmelite, my Mom, and I all graduated high school there in 1919, 1944, and 1978, respectively.

S.S.A. was filled with girls who seemed to be cute, pretty, beautiful, or drop-dead gorgeous. Like most girls of that age, I definitely had my insecurities. The best my mirror ever reflected was "plain". Perhaps I should have bought a new mirror!

Challenged by a teacher one day to think 'What is your best gift from God?' I first thought *Well, it must be intelligence,* because I knew I was fairly smart. Then, the more I thought about it, the more I realized that my best gift from God was my strong faith. Faith is a *gift,* and my faith has helped me survive in ways that my intellect never could have. Even as an adolescent, I knew that my faith was unusually strong – rare, even.

God gave me all the tools I needed to become a writer. My mom, a top-notch English teacher, modeled perfect grammar in our home. Reading classic books as a teenager helped me to know good writing when I saw it – to know what it was supposed to sound like. Being a logophile helped me become a wordsmith; both the written word and the spoken word intrigue me. What also helped nudge my skills along was that my best friend in high school, Lori Calamari, and I would write fifteen page letters to each other *every week* during the summer. Lori lived in Slidell and neither of our families would let us make long distance phone calls because of the expense. A long distance call cost *a fortune* back in the day! But I must say, practicing my writing greatly improved my power of description. Being able to write well is a silent superpower.

My dad was strong, both physically and mentally, and had both common sense and Biblical values. A great businessman, he was friendly and astute. I started working alongside him at the drugstore when I was thirteen years old, and apprenticed there for ten years. It was there that he taught me to "avoid even the appearance of wrong doing".

When I was fifteen, something frustrating happened at the drugstore and I said to Dad, "Well that's not fair!" He stopped me dead in my tracks and said, *"Mary Ann, life is not supposed to be fair."* That was the first time I had ever heard those words spoken aloud and it was a shock to my system. Before that moment, I really believed that life was supposed to be fair.

The wisdom of those seven words helped me to survive cancer. When I was diagnosed in 1992, I had no self pity. I completely understood that invaluable lesson imparted by my dad so many years earlier. My mom's words also resounded in my ears: "Life is not supposed to be perfect. If it were, it would be called heaven." God was preparing me even back then.

At the drugstore, Dad would say quirky things. To combat a stressful situation, he'd say, "We have fun. Tell the truth!" and it always seemed to break the tension. After hearing good news, he'd say, "You can't beat that with a stick! Go get a stick!" But my favorite was after hearing a confusing explanation, he'd say sarcastically, "Well that's about as clear as mud."

My dad was a really funny guy. Customers would come in the drugstore and greet Stanley with a friendly, "Hey! How're ya' doing today?" Dad's response would be, "If it got any better I couldn't stand it!" I like to say that now, even if it's not true, because it makes me feel happy. Dad might ask a regular customer, "How're ya' doing?" and they would respond, "Great!" Dad would immediately follow up with, "You never had a bad day in your life!" and laughter would ensue.

Dad was warm and gregarious. He was certainly an amazing man to work with and taught me a lot. Dad always had an upbeat attitude which he maintains to this day and I was blessed to spend those precious years working alongside him.

In high school, my favorite extracurricular activity – other than seeing how many Oreo cookies I could stuff in a glass of milk – was speech club. Although I competed in Dramatic Interpretation in high schools all over New Orleans, I honestly never was very good at it. I just did it to be with my friends who were in it, one of whom won at nationals! The good news is that I definitely developed some public speaking skills which certainly came in handy later in life. I also went to State Rally in Spanish Interpretation and won first place in state two years in a row. *Hablo un poquito Español! No mucho.*

At sixteen years old, I was allowed to start dating. Dad imposed a strict 11 o'clock curfew but there wasn't much to do in Covington anyway, so it wasn't that bad. My dad was the stereotypical father who stood at the front door flicking the porch light on and off if I lingered past 11:05. Sadly, I wasn't popular enough to give Dad's flicker finger much action.

As a teenager I loved music. My favorite singers were Elton John and Cat Stevens. Later, Lou and I were into bands like Boston, Queen, and Chicago, and singers like Billy Joel, Boz Scaggs, and Peter Frampton. We listened to them on Casey Kasem's American Top 40 which was a big deal back in the day. It was the biggest show on the radio, and we had both AM and FM by then!

English and Math were my strong suits in school. Mom helped me with my English, and Dad with my Math. My earliest memory of Dad stressing the importance of something was when I was in the second grade. Dad was working with me on my times tables and he said, "Mary Ann, there is no excuse for not knowing your times tables. They are simply memorization." Dad then proceeded to drill me every night until I knew them backwards and forwards. All I knew was if it was important to Dad, it was important to me. *That small investment Dad made in my education put me ahead of the curve in math for the rest of my life.*

Despite the importance of Dad's math drills, Mom was my favorite teacher because she taught me so much about life. She made learning fun. Not a day passed that I didn't grow in both knowledge and wisdom; Mom made certain of that. She was wise, gentle, and loving – the perfect mother. Everything Mom said was important because she measured her words carefully. I wish I were more like her in that way, but I realize that I have my own set of gifts. God created me as I am for a reason.

Considering travel an essential part of our education, Mom took me to Europe when I was sixteen years old. We saw eleven countries in twenty-three days, touring a broad swath of Western and Central Europe. I'm so grateful for that trip because it expanded my horizons, broadened my perspective, and enriched my mind.

Mom and Dad frequently shared stories of their childhood with Lou and me and in doing so, emphasized the importance of our family history. In much the same way, the Gospels were passed down orally for decades before they were finally recorded for future generations. This is exactly why I wrote this book – for my children – so that the stories of struggle and faith and the lessons learned from them won't die. My friends Rick and Kally Wyatt call that generational strengthening. *Whatever you learn that sticks with you, pass it on! It's important!* Hopefully this will be my legacy.

Speaking of valuable lessons, as a senior in high school, I once complained to my father, "Dad, I really don't want to go to Mass! I don't get anything out of it!" He said gently, "But Mary Ann, I think God appreciates our attendance even more if we *don't* want to be there. That shows that we are simply there because we love Him." *Wow. Good answer.* I never forgot that. That successfully put my youthful rebellion to rest. *A soft answer does indeed turn away wrath* (Proverbs 15:1).

Chapter Ten

The College Years

After graduating from St. Scholastica Academy, I went to Northeast Louisiana University in Monroe and did two years of pre-pharmacy, then spent three years in pharmacy school there. It was a great experience. Although I didn't know a soul when I entered college, God blessed me with many lifelong friendships that began there.

When I was homesick on Labor Day weekend, Mom, in her infinite wisdom, encouraged me to go check out the Catholic Newman Center where I might make a nice little friend. That's when I met my best friend and mentor, Liz Brinkhaus. We bonded immediately. Karen Brignac was Liz's roommate and the three of us had a great deal in common. I had a lot of fun in college. Getting to stay out past 11:00 was exciting! (Not too exciting because Monroe rolled the sidewalks up at midnight.)

Dating was fun in college, but I also had a blast with all my sisters in Kappa Epsilon, a women's pharmacy fraternity. Our favorite event was the yearly Crush Party that we put on for Valentine's Day. Each girl got to invite two boys and the invitations were sent anonymously. Since none of the guys knew who invited them, they flirted with all the girls. That was my kind of party!

My last year in college, Mom and Dad bought me my first car, a brand new Chevrolet Chevette. It cost $6,300. A Chevy Cavalier replaced that, then I've been a minivan mom ever since. I'm fifty-eight years old now, and only on my fifth car. A word to the wise – making your vehicles last is a good way to save money!

Like most of my friends, I attended Mass faithfully on campus. My funniest experience in church was when I was there with my friend, Tom. The congregation was in the middle of saying the 1700 year old Nicene Creed, having just finished the "I believe in Jesus Christ" section, when Tom absentmindedly said Amen rather loudly, thinking we were at the end. I started giggling and couldn't stop. With a gleam in his eye, Tom leaned over and asked softly, "When did they add that new paragraph to the Creed?" The giggles really burst out after that! I think maybe even my guardian angel was laughing.

In college, Liz in particular inspired me. Wanting to attend daily Mass during Lent, Liz walked a mile and a half in the freezing cold weather to a nearby church in order to attend 6:30am Mass before class. Following her example, I went too. Observing Liz's gentle heart and devotion to Christ in the Eucharist, I found that I began to change for the better. Many a sunny afternoon was spent relaxing on the banks of Bayou Desiard, reading <u>My Daily Bread</u> Father Anthony Paone and pondering the meaning of life. I found a Bible verse that sums up the friendship I have with Liz.

"A faithful friend is a sturdy shelter. He who finds one finds a treasure. A faithful friend is beyond price. No sum can balance his worth. A faithful friend is a life-saving remedy, such as he who fears God finds; for he who fears God will behave accordingly, and his friend will be like himself" (Sirach 6:14-17).

Chapter Eleven
My New Home

After graduating from college in May 1983, I moved to Lafayette, Louisiana. In college, all of my friends were from Cajun country, and that whole area intrigued me. The people in Lafayette were warm and friendly, welcoming me graciously into the fold. This is now where I call home.

I met my future husband, Jeff, that summer. He a pharmacist with my friend Karen Brignac at K-Mart. Karen would always tell me, "You should meet my partner, Jeff. I really think you would like him!" Then she would tell Jeff, "You should meet my friend, Mary Ann. I really think you would like her!" Our first meeting was when about twenty K-mart employees went out after work to a bar named Poets and they invited me to go. Jeff and I hit it off immediately.

The next day, I got a dozen red roses with a note saying, "Will you go out with me? J." Jeff laughed as he said, "I thought if you couldn't figure out who J was, then you probably weren't interested in dating me." But I knew *exactly* who it was and we went on our first date that weekend. After that, Jeff sent me flowers every month in an attempt to woo my heart. When we married two years later, I urged him, "Honey, you have to stop sending me flowers! They are *too expensive*! We have to save our money." Jeff, with a twinkle in his blue eyes, would just laugh.

After Jeff and I had been dating a few months, he insisted that I memorize Scripture including the book, chapter, and verse. That way, I'd know where to find it in the Bible – its address, so to speak. The first one he taught me was Proverbs 3:5-6: *"Trust in the Lord with all your heart and lean not unto your own understanding. In all your ways acknowledge Him, and He will direct your paths."* Having those wise words in my memory bank helped calm me in many a stressful time. Memorizing Scripture is loading time-tested, workable wisdom into your moral G.P.S., so that you can always find your way home when you're lost.

Jeff was a very good sport. He always liked my cooking even though I didn't really know how to cook when we got married. The first time I made crawfish étouffée, I mistakenly thought that the proportion between onion and bell pepper was one to one, rather than one onion to half a bell pepper. My crawfish étouffée came out green! Well, Jeff ate every bite and even went back for seconds. Julia Child, I am not.

Jeff sang tenor in several different barbershop quartets, including The Bayou Blend and The Louisiana Purchase. Singing was his great passion, so we traveled together to barbershop competitions, even attending nationals one year in Atlanta. Jeff's particular favorite was the singing Valentines they delivered each year on Valentine's Day. Laughingly he said, "It's the only day of the year where I can sing a love song to another man's wife and not get in trouble for it."

One of Jeff and my earliest vacations together was to Nashville, where among other things we went to the iconic theme park, Opryland. They had a show for almost every genre of music imaginable. Well, no surprise here, my favorite was a delightful musical version of an Old West show called "Way Out West." It was complete with singing and dancing cowboys and bar maids, a tall, handsome sheriff, bank robbers, and the townspeople – including this pretty little girl, with a big bow in her long blonde hair, holding a giant lollipop. That "little girl" was the best singer I had ever heard in my life; I was stunned to hear that caliber of talent at a theme park.

Jeff and I went back to every single performance that day, not simply to see this delightful production, but to watch a budding star in the making. I really sensed I was in the presence of greatness. After the second performance, we introduced ourselves to the young lady. She was just nineteen years old and, away from home for the summer, was terribly homesick. A sweet, bubbly girl named Kristi, she said that we reminded her of her parents back home in Oklahoma. We visited for a good while after every show, six in all, and had a surprisingly touching exchange of emotions, receiving many hugs. I was so impressed with her talent that I gave her our home address and phone number and told her, "Kristi, you are going to be a big star on Broadway one day, and when you are, I hope you will let Jeff and me know. We will fly up to New York see you, because we really believe in you." The next day we left Nashville, quickly putting aside our wonderful encounter with our new friend in the busyness of our day-to-day lives.

Twenty-five years later, I was cleaning out my house and came across an old map of Opryland. Recalling the young teen fondly, I flipped to the back of the map where she had signed her name, Kristi Chenoweth. I knew it! Even as a nineteen year old, her talent was blatantly obvious even to the most casual of observers. Her voice, with no microphone, filled the entire outdoor theatre. It was an honor and a privilege to have witnessed her talent early on.

When I became a new mother, I had never even changed a diaper before. Hoping to become a good parent, I went to the library and checked out every single book on parenting, determined to do it to the best of my abilities. My goal from a young age was to raise happy, healthy, well mannered children who had every advantage that I could offer them. (Success!) We were blessed with three beautiful children, Greg, the oldest, Amy, the only girl, and Matthew, the baby. Fortunately in our family, we had no "middle child." Jeff was a wonderful father and his volunteering in scouting and Project CHARLIE, the in-school drug and alcohol prevention program, was a powerful influence on our children. Jeff doted on the kids and instilled in them a love of sports and nature.

One year, during the six weeks of Lent, we decided that we would give up television. Greg, at four and Amy, at two enjoyed the time filled with outdoor play, reading, and board games. We made the same sacrifice a second time when Greg was nine, Amy was seven, and Matthew was three. Board games changed from Chutes and Ladders and Candyland, to Clue and Sorry! There was more outdoor play with basketball games like HORSE and Knock Out, and as always, time was set aside for adventures in reading. However, because the kids were older, giving up TV was a bit harder on them. Greg told me that he never wanted to do it again, because March Madness was in Lent and he hated missing all the basketball games. That being said, we bonded greatly as a family and created many happy memories.

Because of my cancer, Greg was forced to grow up at a very young age. At seven years old, he would empty the dishwasher to help out around the house. Once, when the radiation treatments had me so nauseated that I couldn't get out of bed, Greg opened a can of ravioli and heated it up for Amy in the microwave. When she was finished, Amy ran into my bedroom and before I could stop her, put her artificial orange, ravioli-covered hands on my new seafoam green comforter. Hearing my long inward gasp of horror and seeing the shocked look on my face set my precious five year old's wheels turning. "Bedeep! Bedeep! Bedeep! That's all folks!" came out. I just burst out laughing and all the tension melted away. Comforters can be replaced.

One Saturday morning when the kids were young, they were all piled up on one beanbag chair watching cartoons. I walked to my bedroom for a moment, and when I came back, Greg and Amy were still sitting on the beanbag chair, eyes glued to the set, but Matthew completely had disappeared. *Oh no!* I thought, *Gone for one minute and I lost a child!* Quickly, I searched the house before asking, "Where on earth is Matthew?" The kids replied in unison, "Under the beanbag chair!" Sure enough! Between the tangled mix of legs and buried underneath the beanbag chair, was the little freckle-faced redhead, watching cartoons. That's why that boy is so darned tough! It's amazing they didn't kill him!

Matthew was always a very generous child. Once when he was in preschool, I gave him his 25 cents allowance and he immediately said, "Oh boy, Mom! For 25 cents I can get four pieces of gum at Mr. Al's Barber Shop – two for Greg, one for Amy, and one for me." AWWWWW!

One summer when we were on vacation in Gulf Shores, our family spent the day on the beach and then went out for pizza. After returning to the hotel, where the five of us were staying in one room, Jeff and I decided to sit on the balcony and listen to the waves while the children got ready for bed. We barely had a moment to relax when the smoke alarm went off in the room. I immediately ran inside, picturing the room burning down with our children in it. There was black smoke billowing out of the microwave oven. Four year old Matthew had brought home a small square of pizza from the pizza place, carefully wrapped in a dirty, crumpled, brown paper napkin. Apparently, he had put the pizza in the microwave and pressed five minutes, setting the pizza on fire and leaving a blackened, charred mess. While Jeff cleaned up the mess, I went over to console a sad and sobbing Matthew.

I hugged him tightly and said reassuringly, "It's okay, honey! You didn't burn the room down".

And he said, with his little voice quivering through the tears, "I knooowww! *But I really wanted that piece of pizza!*"

I would greatly encourage you to write down those funny things your children say. They bring us so much pleasure and we think we'll remember them forever, but memories fade. It's important to a family's unity to always remember the good times.

Chapter Twelve

The Children

When our kids were young, some of their happiest times were the summers spent outdoors, playing with our next door neighbors Nick and Natalie Domino. They would all play hide and seek over our two yards. One time, I came home from an errand and found a note taped to the cabinet saying "Mom, I'm over playing at Nick and Natalie's house. Nobody kidnapped me. Don't worry. Love, Greg."

Working full-time as a pharmacist, I treasured my days off with my family. Every year, a week of my vacation time was earmarked for the children's first week of school. When the kids got off the bus, I had fresh baked cookies or brownies and soft drinks spread on a picnic blanket on the driveway. All the other kids on the bus were jealous as my three raced off to join Nick, Natalie, and Mitzi for snacks and conversation. That was so much fun! For me, hearing about my children's day was one of life's greatest pleasures.

Jeff was instrumental in giving our boys the support they needed to earn the rank of Eagle Scout. He was there every step of the way, particularly with Matthew. Starting as a leader in Tiger

Cubs in the first grade and continuing into the teenage years when they achieved the honor of Eagle Scout, Jeff was as actively involved as he could possibly be while working full-time. Matthew said that his favorite memories of his dad came from scouting.

"He was there," Matthew emphasized. "That's all it took! Scouting was a very good experience," Matt continued. "It taught me a lot of useful skills. I learned to cook. I gained independence. I was active and out in nature. It was great!" Both of our boys are outdoorsmen because of Boy Scouts.

Jeff and I both worked very hard to provide a nice living for our family, and unfortunately, that included working many nights. When the children were in elementary school, if our whole family had the rare opportunity to sit down together for dinner, it was a cherished occasion. Three candles would be lit, one for each child to blow out, and everyone would contribute to the conversation talking about their day or about whatever they wanted.

One autumn night, our family was chatting when Amy chimed in with, "Number four said no dogs allowed!"

Baffled, we all looked at Amy, quietly waiting for further explanation, but our sweet eight-year-old just continued eating. Not sure I heard correctly, I gently asked, *"Honey, what did you say?"*

Confidently, Amy repeated, "Number four said no dogs allowed!"

Confused, I asked, "What does that mean, Amy?"

Our precious daughter replied, "Remember how this summer we went to Blue Bayou Water Park?"

"Yeeess," I said slowly, not sure where this was headed.

"Well, outside the park they had a sign listing the rules and number four said, 'No dogs allowed!'"

Wow! I didn't see that one coming! I guess she wondered why the dogs couldn't get in on all the fun, like in the classic children's book, "Go, Dog. Go!" In that moment, my third grade cutie-pie established herself as the memory champion of the Fontenot family. That story still brings a smile to my face.

With her love of dogs, Amy reminds me of myself when I was young. I once asked Mama, "Mom, can dogs go to heaven?" Mom gently replied, "No honey. They don't have a soul." Thinking about that for a moment, I said, "But Mama, how can it be heaven if they don't allow dogs?" Touché!

Turning off the television revolutionized the way I parented. Empowered by the concept that I could gain control of our household by turning off the TV, I quickly put that theory to the test. Our children became much better readers, their standardized test scores improved, and we became a much closer family because of it. Armed with that information, I started a "Donate a Book" program at Our Lady of Fatima School where all the parents donated a book to their child's classroom library. I believe that reading is key to a strong future, not only for our children, but for our country. This "Donate a Book" program was very easy to set up. I simply had each teacher compile a list of age appropriate literature for the children to pick from and the child then asked their parents to donate one hardcover book. By the following week, thirty new books were in each classroom!

Mitzi Domino once said something very profound to me that I will never forget. One day, I had something on my mind and I needed to talk, so I walked next door to see my friend and mentor. At that time, Mitzi and two other moms, Reneé Bennett and Marvita Hudson, were in the process of creating The Children's Museum of Acadiana. Together, they came up with the idea, found the location, acquired financing, planned every section in there, and got sponsorships for the exhibits. Mitzi and her friends also spent months collecting and putting together children's handprints on tiles as a major fundraiser from the community. This particular day, I could barely see Mitzi over the huge pile of paperwork on the table and instinctively I apologized, saying, "Oh Mitzi! I'm so sorry! Am I catching you at a bad time?" I will never forget her response. She said, "I am never too busy to nurture a friendship." Wow! *I am never too busy to nurture a friendship.*

While Mitzi was inside working on The Children's Museum, Greg was next door spending hours and hours practicing basketball. One summer afternoon, I was waiting for a washer repairman to come. Ten year old Greg wanted to go to Red's Health Club to a find a pickup game of basketball, but he discovered that his bike had a flat tire. He asked me to bring him, but I explained that I couldn't leave the house. Intent on playing that day, Greg walked the three miles to the gym dribbling his basketball the entire way. Greg was determined, even at a young age.

Later that year, Greg's Biddy Basketball team made it to the world championship tournament in Tulsa, Oklahoma. Even though Greg usually sat the bench, he was by far the best free throw shooter on the team, so his coach entered him into the free throw competition. Now this contest was held over the course of four days, so in the early stages, he competed only once a day. Before we left our hotel room each day, we would pray as a family, and each time, Greg advanced to the next round. The last day, after winning several rounds, Greg made it to the finals.

Determined to continue our family tradition, Jeff, Greg, and I found a quiet place in the gym under the bleachers to pray. Before we began, Greg quietly asked, "Mom, don't you think that the other boy is praying to win too? I mean what is God going to do with both of us praying to win?" I assured him quickly, "Oh honey! We are not praying that you win, we are praying that you *do your best*, and I'm *certain* that if you do your best, you will win."

The final free throw competition was the best of 25 shots. Greg's opponent won the toss, so he shot first and made 4/5. Greg quickly answered back with 4/5. Then they switched the order and Greg sunk 4/5 and the other boy answered in kind. After the third round, they were in a dead heat. The cheers in the gym grew louder as all eyes focused on the two sharpshooters. Greg was up and he swished five in a row! The pressure was on. Could that ten year old boy keep up with the mighty Greg Fontenot? (Whoops! Sorry! I lost myself in the moment.) He could not, making only three of his five shots. After the last round, the young competitor was still in the game, and his team and fans were determined to influence the outcome. Greg was the last to walk up to the free-throw line. Bounce, bounce, bounce came Greg's familiar routine. The roar behind the basket was deafening – so loud in fact that you couldn't even hear the swish as Greg brought the trophy home!

Greg had practiced every day for three years, rain or shine. He ended up shooting 84% on his free throws that day, better even than Michael Jordan's average of 83%! Greg may have been declared "world champion", but he gained so much more than that. He learned firsthand the *power of prayer* and *the immeasurable value of hard work and dedication.* That's a lesson that has stuck with him for life.

My having grown up with depression era parents whose families struggled to make ends meet left a marked impression on me. As a result, I had a hard time justifying splurges on myself. One big splurge that I *could* justify was buying a brand spanking new Dodge Grand Caravan. Having three kids now, I needed a bigger and safer vehicle than my old Chevy Cavalier to haul them around. That being said, after much prayer and discussion, Jeff and I decided that even though as two full-time pharmacists, we could certainly afford a new van, it would cut into our budget enough to take away our little splurges on our children. That, to us, was not worth it. The next day we returned the van to the dealership. Wistfully, I got my economy car back and drove home. That night, we took the kids out and drowned our sorrows in pizza. There's always a silver lining in every cloud. Keep that in mind.

Right before my second cancer surgery, my mother had been diagnosed with breast cancer, so she couldn't be with me as she had for my first. In order to encourage me to fight, Mom promised, "If we survive this, I will take you on a life affirming trip anywhere you want to go in the United States." Well, I had the feeding tube in for almost a year, and then it took another year to get strong enough to take a long trip, but finally two years later, I took Mom up on her offer. Surprisingly, she said, "You know Mary Ann, I am too old for an active sightseeing trip, so I would like to give the trip to you and Jeff." Excited for a little getaway, we originally planned to go to New York City, but Mom suggested Washington D.C. and, for some reason, that idea piqued my interest.

Jeff and I went to Washington D.C. in December 1995. We had every night planned in advance; however, a month before our trip, our dinner cruise on the Potomac fell through, leaving a night open. When we got to D.C., we bought a newspaper which had all of the evening's activities listed. Jeff and I narrowed the dozens of options down to three. We were either going to see a play at the American Theatre, a murder mystery at the Kennedy Center, or Scrooge at Ford's Theatre where Lincoln was shot. We settled on the murder mystery: Jeff was interested in seeing the Kennedy Center and I had always wanted to see a murder mystery play.

Walking into the small theater, we saw that we had bought the last two tickets. They handed us a Playbill and in it, was an opportunity to purchase a raffle ticket as a fundraiser for the National Symphony Orchestra. The grand prize was a Mercedes-Benz. Strange as this may seem, I turned to Jeff and said excitedly, "Let's do this Jeff! I can win a car! My dad won a Lincoln back in 1974." High hopes? Perhaps. But that is me. It's in my DNA. Several weeks later, the ticket arrived by mail and it was number 199. I exclaimed, "Jeff, do you realize our odds of winning the Mercedes? There have been less than 200 tickets sold! I'm going to buy another one."

Well, the second ticket that I bought, number 736, was the winning ticket. I'd just won a brand new Benz!

For the car fans among you, the Mercedes Benz I won in 1996 was their newest model, the E320. It was in such high demand at the time that there were none to be had in the United States, anywhere. Mine was custom ordered from the factory in Germany. I chose their most popular color, silver, and then sold it

103

back to the local dealership that had a list of people waiting to buy one. I never even drove it. You see, I am not a car person. I'm too practical for that. Once Moss Motors cut me that check, I had enough money to pay cash for the Dodge Grand Caravan that I had returned four months earlier, pay for our trip back to Washington D.C. to attend the reception in my honor, and cover the income taxes on my winnings. My children called it "the van that God gave us." Indeed!

On our return trip to Washington D.C. for the reception, the ladies in charge of the fundraiser took us out to lunch. Jeff told them about my courageous battle with cancer and my unexpected survival. "It's a really good story!" Jeff bragged. "You should have her tell y'all", which I did. That evening, we attended a performance of the National Symphony Orchestra where we had box seats with our new friends. During the intermission was the reception in my honor and they asked me to speak. That was the first time I gave my testimony. Moved by my story of faith, many people came up to me after my talk, telling me how much I inspired them. Apparently I struck a universal chord; I even received letters back home, thanking me for sharing my faith.

I like to think back on all the things that had to fall in place for this moment to happen. If we had gone to New York City rather than to Washington D.C., we wouldn't have been in the right place at the right time. If our plans hadn't fallen through for the river cruise, we wouldn't have had an open night. If we hadn't gotten the last two tickets to the play, we wouldn't have had the opportunity to buy the raffle tickets. If I hadn't bought the second raffle ticket, we wouldn't have won the car. All of this was much more than a coincidence, it was a God-incidence, leading me not just to win the Mercedes, but to give my testimony of God's love, mercy, and faithfulness. You see, *it was never about winning a car*. I honestly feel that God had His hand in my life, leading me to where He wanted me to go. "And we know that in all things God works for the good of those who love Him, who have been called according to His purpose" (Romans 8:28).

The day before Thanksgiving in 1997, a tornado hit my hometown of Covington. About two in the afternoon, Dad was leaving to go to the Goodwill store to drop off a few things. Mom walked him to the door and Dad got as far as his car, before the sky suddenly got very dark and the wind picked up significantly.

"Honey, why don't you wait awhile to go? It looks really bad out there," Mom urged.

Well, by the time it took Dad to get up the stairs and into the house, the tell-tale sound of a freight train was roaring and Dad, using all his might, could barely get the door shut. Running to the hallway, Daddy and Mama lay side by side, Dad's arm around Mom to protect her from harm. A huge pine tree crashed through the bathroom wall, demolishing everything right up to the hall where my parents lay, but thank God, they were untouched. In all, fourteen trees fell on their property, with three of them hitting the house.

Lou was driving home for Thanksgiving that day, and he could barely recognize the neighborhood he grew up in. Mama had put a candle in the window to let Lou know that everything was okay. Because of all the renovations, Mom and Dad were out of their home for over six months. Houses can be replaced. There are two ways to view every tragedy. You can ask, "Why me, Lord? Why did this have to happen to me?" Or you can ask, "Why me, Lord? Why am I so blessed as to have survived this?" The choice is ours.

The kids will all tell you that their favorite Christmas was the year that we got our dog Spot. Amy is most proud because she named him. This squirmy little, black-and-white spotted rat terrier puppy, barely six weeks old, was in a box that we had pre-wrapped and put a bow on. When the children opened the box, the first thing Amy said was, "Spot! His name is Spot!" Greg was disappointed because he wanted to name him Charlie, but Amy got dibs and Spot it was.

Looking back on my childhood, one of the most meaningful things that my Mom ever did was becoming room mother for my class. It meant so much to me that she was involved. That's why I always tried to be there for our three kids because I knew it was important, I knew how special it was to me as a child. Therefore, every game, every dance revue, every play, Jeff and I were always there. Our kids were always our top priority and we would work as many twelve hour days as necessary to be off for their events.

One summer day, Mrs. Isabelle, our beloved, long time housekeeper was hard at work making our messy house livable again. Before she began mopping the floor, Isabelle told the kids, "The floor is wet. Y'all be careful." A few minutes later, eight year old Amy saw the mailman pass and came scooting out of her room. Pffffft. Boom! Amy hit the floor with a thud. Her screams could be heard from two doors down. Isabelle told me she immediately thought, "I'm going to jail! They are going to arrest me for child abuse! What am I going to do?" Ten year old Greg rushed out and came to the rescue. Isabelle said that he immediately took charge of the situation, calming Amy and assuring her that she was going to be fine. Then he calmed *Isabelle* and assured *her* that it was going to be fine. Now that Greg is a doctor, Isabelle says she could see that caretaker side of him even when he was young.

The name Amy means "greatly loved" or "beloved." Well, one memorable gift I gave my beloved daughter for her eleventh birthday was a journal. Knowing that those tough junior high years can be so damaging to your self-esteem, I wanted to bolster my child's self-image before she entered them. I took that journal to every relative, school teacher, dance teacher, friend, godparent, and neighbor – even the principal and the bus driver – and they all wrote a short message wishing Amy a happy birthday and telling her how special she was. The affirmations of love from every person she knew helped form my precious brown eyed girl into the wonderful young lady she is today.

One weekend, Jeff had taken Amy swimming, Greg had gone to the library for research, and Matthew, who was about eight at the time, was out playing with his friends in the neighborhood. So having some time to myself, I decided to take a nap. I was awakened by the sound of a child's footsteps treading on the carpet. It was Matthew. He walked towards me with a paperback book in his hands. "Mom! Miss Karen gave Joel and me each a quarter to buy something at the garage sale down the street, so I bought you this book! The lady told me that it was a really good book, so I'm going get another quarter from my bank to buy you another one." *AWWWW! How thoughtful! The lady told him it was a really good book, so he wanted to buy me another one!* (You just can't beat that with a stick! Go get a stick!)

I remember the first time I discovered that Matthew could sing. In the fourth grade, he came home from school and said, "Mom, we learned a new song at school today and it goes like this: 'DAY-O! DAY AY AY O! Daylight come and me wanna go home.'" We were standing in the kitchen and the windows shook! *Literally!* I just couldn't believe that big booming voice came out of that little bitty boy. Inconceivable! (To steal a quote from one of our favorite movies, *The Princess Bride.*)

Matthew joined the cross country team at school in the fifth grade and the following is an email I sent to a friend after his first big race: "Matthew ran his first big race this Saturday. I was so proud I had tears in my eyes. He completed the entire two miles, and although he was among the youngest (ranging from 5th to 8th grade), he finished about midway. *I* was so proud! *He* was so proud! Long distance racing is truly an event of human drama, of mind over matter, of the human spirit triumphing over the human body." So true.

At Our Lady of Fatima, Amy was in the pep squad for two years before becoming a cheerleader in the 8th grade. Cheering for her school's football team, especially against their local rivals, was thrilling to Amy. After the game, the winning team would head over to Judice Inn, the iconic local burger joint that's been around since the 1940s. There, the football players and the cheerleaders squeezed into the dozen or so booths, celebrating jubilantly while their parents stood around chatting and reveling in the moment, recalling their own "good ole days." Burgers and milkshakes after the big game have been a tradition for many generations.

Chapter Thirteen

Faith

When I was teaching Confirmation in 2010, I gave the following speech on The Nicene Creed.

The first line in the Nicene Creed is: *We believe in one God, the Father, the Almighty, maker of heaven and earth, of all that is seen and unseen.*

"Is God Almighty?" I believe! But let me share a story with you that highlights the creative genius of God and I'll let you decide for yourselves.

Ten years ago, I had the privilege of spending a few weeks with a decorated war hero from WWII, a man named Mike Simpson. Mike's very first combat experience was on Utah Beach, one of the five beaches in Normandy attacked on D-Day. You'll remember that the success of D-Day, the biggest military invasion in history, began the end of Nazi terror that held Western Europe captive.

Mike's memories were painful – horrific memories of blood, death, and destruction. You see, Mike was a medic. His job was to dispense morphine to the wounded and to comfort the dying, all amidst the terrifying roar of gunfire and bombs. So many of these young men were only twenty-one or twenty-two. Mike and the other medics worked seventy-two hours straight with no sleep and little food. The things Mike saw in those gruesome days would haunt him for decades. He had nightmares that seemed never ending.

After the war, Mike married a wonderful woman named Mary and had two sons. In 1976, the Simpsons' oldest son, John, was twenty-five and living on his own in Colorado when he fell in love with a girl named Claudia. In time, Mike and Mary flew out to Colorado for their son's wedding, meeting Claudia and her parents.

Realizing that Claudia's Dad, Joe, was about his own age, Mike shifted the conversation to WWII. "Did you serve in the war?"

"Yes, actually, I did," came the reply.

Mike smiled, "Me, too. I was part of the D-Day invasion of Normandy."

Joe said, "I was in Normandy as well."

Incredulous, Mike continued, "I was in the attack on Utah Beach."

Grimfaced, Joe said, "I was on Utah Beach too.... I was defending it."

Mike told me there was a long pause as the two men pondered the gravity of what had just transpired.

Joe was a pre-teen student in Germany who simply joined an after school club. In that innocent environment, Hitler began to indoctrinate the youth of Germany with Nazi propaganda. After the war,

Joe and his family moved to Chicago, but Joe never let his children join any extra-curricular activities.

For Mike, his developing friendship with Joe and learning the fact that he and many others like him were just innocent kids duped by an evil man began to rid him of his nightmares. Within a few weeks, they disappeared completely. So you tell me. *Is God, Almighty? I believe!*

At the beginning of another Confirmation class, we indulged in a sensory experience which seemed to resonate with the kids. I had two beautiful red roses in a vase on my desk. Halfway through the hour, I passed one rose around the room and each student pulled a petal off. In one word, they had to describe a single facet of the flower –color, texture, scent, etc. At the end of the hour, the rose that was used and passed around was drooping – stem broken and petals stripped. The other was fresh, vibrant and whole. I then told the sixteen year olds, "Think of the rose as your body. Make wise choices."

One day I was outside weeding my flower bed, and as I dug deep in the dirt to get to the roots of the weeds, it occurred to me how much weeds are like sin. If you get them out when you first notice them, they're very easy to remove. However, if you wait, the roots grow deeper and stronger and the weeds become extremely difficult to get rid of.

When my mother had her cancer relapse eight years after her initial diagnosis, I quickly realized that this Christmas may be her last with us. Hoping that Christmas carols would cheer Mom up, I worked up a little program where Jeff, who had a beautiful tenor voice, sang some carols solo, we all sang as a family, and the children sang a few together. Ten year old Matthew was the only child who had a solo, singing "Mary Did You Know".

At the end of the concert, Jeannie pulled me aside and said, "Wow, Mary Ann! Matthew *really can sing!* I know *everybody* thinks their grandchildren can sing, and the others sing *okay*, but Matthew *is really talented.*"

It warms my heart that Jeannie knew what a great singer Matt was before she died. Thank you God! Jeanne Marie LeBlanc Bridges died on January 29, 2002, Dad re-married on Valentine's Day 2004. After being happily married to my mom for forty-nine and a half years, Dad is almost fifteen years into his second marriage to a kind-hearted woman named Frances. Go, Dad!

I had a very blessed childhood. Mom was an absolute saint. When she died, her priest confessor, Fr. Thomas, told me he thought she *was* a saint. He said, "When *Jeanne* came to confession, *I* felt better!" Whoa! I can't even imagine!

I had never heard Mama say a bad word about anybody, ever. I think that's one of the things that drew me to Liz and Karen in college and bonded our friendship. They were very much like my mama in that way. I miss my mom to this day.

In the spring of Greg's junior year at St. Thomas More, Mr. Roy Petitfils walked up to Greg and asked, "Hey, Greg! Why don't you go with us on the mission trip to Mexico over the Easter break?"

Greg replied, "Nah, Mr. P. That's really not my thing."

The next day Mr. P. came up to Greg a second time and urged, "Greg, I really think you need to go on this mission trip. Why don't you go? It'll be fun!"

A second time Greg said, "Nah, Mr. P. I'm really not interested. Thank you though."

The third day once again, Mr. Petitfils came up to Greg and challenged him by saying, "Greg, I really think the Holy Spirit is calling your name. Why don't you go on this mission trip with us?"

So Greg prayed about it and decided to go.

When Greg came back from that mission trip in Mexico he stunned me with these words, "Mom, I have found my mission in life, and it is in hard labor for the underprivileged." I remember being flabbergasted that a boy that age – he was sixteen at the time – could make such a profound life statement. I was so blown away that I wrote it down in my journal.

Since that time, Greg has gone on three mission trips and served a year in the Jesuit Volunteer Corps in Boise, Idaho. In med school, Greg opted for the Rural Scholars Track, choosing to help fill the dire need for family practice physicians in rural Louisiana. That week in Mexico provided both a blueprint and foundation for his life. Thanks Roy!

For Jeff's fiftieth birthday, I gave him a trip to New York City. Neither of us had ever been, and we were both looking forward to it. Our celebratory vacation was planned for September 20, 2001.

Then 9/11 happened.

Time stopped in America. We all remember where we were when we witnessed this terrible tragedy. Our country mourned in solidarity. As far as our trip was concerned, we just didn't know if it was feasible. Airlines didn't get back to a full running flight schedule until the Monday before our Thursday departure. Many people cancelled their travel plans out of fear of more terrorism. Broadway almost went bankrupt. We weren't sure if the shows we held tickets for would be up and running yet. All that being said, I knew I wasn't going to let fear run my life – so I talked Jeff into going.

The mood in New York City was obviously very somber. Several large security guards at the entrance of the Waldorf-Astoria checked our ID every time we entered the hotel. Jeff and I had the trip of a lifetime, punctuated by devastation and great sadness. We felt very safe in Manhattan because there was security everywhere.

Our first night there we saw *The Lion King*, the most amazingly beautiful display of artistry I have ever seen in my life. What a way to kick things off! The next day we toured the city on a double-decker bus and walked around the neighborhoods. We saw many firehouses covered with hundreds of bouquets of flowers, thank you notes from children, and gifts of appreciation.

Heart wrenching posters were stapled to telephone poles – "Have you seen this man? Last seen on the 101st floor…Beloved father of three young children…Desperately seeking information!… Please call…." Wooden fences were completely covered with thousands of post-it notes from people pouring out their raw emotions. I cannot imagine the horror.

Later that evening, Jeff and I went out for dinner and dancing at the Rainbow Room, on the 65th floor of the Rockefeller Center. Our evening was poignant and magical: poignant because we could see the site of the World Trade Center, which, nine days after the incident, was still smoking, magical because Jeff and I had the time of our lives. We held each other extra close as we danced to our favorite big band hits.

Everywhere we went, people were talking about 9/11 and what they were doing when it happened. In the restroom, one lady told me that she was at work in Manhattan and her husband was at home in Brooklyn when the planes hit. They couldn't get in touch with one another because cell service was out. Public transportation was completely shut down, so she had no option but to walk home across the Brooklyn Bridge, in high heels. Thousands of people were doing the same thing, everyone scurrying in different directions to get home to their loved ones. Unbeknownst to this lady, her husband, too worried to wait at home for his wife, had gotten on his bicycle with a pair of roller blades around his neck and set out looking for her. She told me that they met up on the Brooklyn Bridge and he gave her the bike and he skated home.

At the end of this very special evening, we were crossing the lobby of our hotel and saw a group of firemen who had worked all day at the rubble. Watching these heroes come in from their physically and emotionally draining work, filthy and exhausted, yet fulfilled – witnessing such a turning point in our county's history is something Jeff and I will never forget. Seeing everyone pull together in this time of crisis made me proud to be an American. We made a point of walking over and shaking their hands, thanking them for their service. God Bless America – land that I love!

My second near-death experience happened in 2004 when I had a routine hysterectomy and was in the hospital recovering after surgery. Jeff was with me when the children, now teenagers, came to the hospital to visit. Everything was fine at that point. After a short visit, the kids went home for lunch, and Jeff went downstairs to grab a quick bite to eat. The rest of the story was relayed to me by my nurse, Karen Bernard, who was my angel in white.

Karen told me, "I normally check up on my patients every hour on the hour, but at 3:40, I had this *overwhelming feeling* that I should go check up on you early. When I got there, your lips were blue, your nail beds were blue, your blood pressure was 70/30, and your respirations were six per minute (normal is 20/minute). You had the death rales – you were gasping for air – so we began CPR."

Jeff, completely unsettled, went on to explain, "Mary Ann! They shook your shoulders! They yelled your name! They drew blood to see if they could figure out what was wrong. They even beat on your chest, but you were lifeless." After twenty minutes, Jeff heard one nurse turn to the other and say, "I think we're losing her."

Immediately after that, my eyes fluttered open. By that time, the room was packed with medical personnel responding to the code blue, every one of them staring at me. Thinking I had just awoken from a nap, I was startled, wondering, *why are all these people in my room watching me sleep???*

When Jeff told me all that had transpired, I simply didn't believe him, insisting "Jeff, if they had taken blood – if they had stuck a needle in my arm – I would know it!" Looking down, I was *shocked*! There in the crook of my arm was the tell-tale bandage bringing clearly into focus just how narrowly I had escaped death.

The next day, Karen told me, "You know, I'm a praying woman, and before every shift I pray that the Lord will lead me where I need to go. In that moment I got an *overwhelming feeling* that I should check up on you early. If I had not come when I did, you would have died. You would not have lasted twenty more minutes."

Yet again, escaping death had a profound effect on me. God keeps having me beat almost insurmountable odds to keep on living. What is it that God wants from me? Where is He directing me?

The summer following his eighth grade year, Matthew told Jeff and me that he wanted to go on a mission trip to Mexico with the youth group from a church parish across town. He had been meeting with the youth group for several months for prayer and worship, but when he told us that he wanted to go out of the country with people I'd never met before, I was shocked. I knew I wasn't going to let our fourteen year old son go to Mexico – in political unrest at the time – without me. Jeff and I discussed it, and we both decided to go as chaperones. Matt, of course, was indignant.

I was terrified to go. Having immense fear of the unknown and many fairly serious health issues, I was concerned to be out of the country, out of my comfort zone, and away from American healthcare. That being said, the Holy Spirit made it crystal clear that I was being called to go. Darn it!

We met with another couple who was also going on the mission trip and as we discussed it, I began to visibly tremble. My mind raced with reasons I should not go. I had no saliva, would I have access to clean water? I had terrible reflux, would the spicy food make me sick? I had insomnia, would I be able to sleep sharing a room with several other women? Would Mexico be safe? How would I handle being on a sixteen hour bus ride with twenty high school aged kids? Yikes! All these things weighed heavily on my mind, but still I felt compelled to go. Not wanting to miss out on a life changing moment with our son, I heard my voice agree to go. Jeff and I were committed.

The bus ride turned out to be delightful! What I feared would be tiresome and nerve-wracking was an adventure in the discovery of stories and souls. Those young people were all faith-filled, pure, and selfless kids and it was a privilege to travel with them. Many were singers who sang Christian songs for a good deal of the way, which really served to pass the time. Once we got past the border, where wiry men with machine guns checked our passports and checked under our bus, the rest of the journey was peaceful and pleasant. We watched several movies, my favorite being <u>Molokai</u> where I learned about Father Damien and the lepers. I felt the Holy Spirit's presence with me because the food did not upset my reflux, I slept like a baby, and once we got past the policemen with machine guns, the trip was not scary at all.

The most powerful experience on that trip came one night at Eucharist Adoration. There were about twenty-five people on their knees worshiping in a small room. Even though I had never previously been moved during Eucharist Adoration, this time I was overwhelmed with emotion and began to sob uncontrollably for about ten minutes. Matthew was right beside me, so I put my arm around his shoulders, hugged him, and told him I loved him. It was a tender reconciling moment between mother and child that only God could have orchestrated.

Our mission trip was part service, part education, and part retreat. Every day there was time for introspection, which was both uplifting and fruitful. Our journey taught me things about life and faith that have continued to serve as a catalyst to my own spiritual growth and change. When we sit across from people and engage them in deep conversation, we are interacting with their very soul. We must look beyond their haircut, their accent, and the color of their outer shell. The sharing of a soul is a sacred thing.

In Mexico, I discovered a piece of myself that I didn't even know was missing – gratitude. Using wet wipe after wet wipe to clean a little girl's hands, ultimately emptying the package before removing the dirt, made me appreciate running water and a bar of soap. Eating lettuce, beans, and cheese everyday made me appreciate the abundant produce available in our local grocery stores. The barren landscape of the area made me appreciate our thick green grass, shade providing trees, and colorful azalea bushes back home.

I was astounded by what I learned in five days – about another land, another culture, another people, simple but proud. Seeing the beautiful Mexican children playing in the dusty road, barefoot yet happy, made me re-evaluate my priorities and free myself from a lot of attachments when I got home. Our mission trip taught me what true humility looks like. It was eye opening to learn the difference between saying, "Why do you do it that way?" which can create defensiveness and divisiveness, and, "Help me understand the reason you do it like that." which creates openness and cooperation.

For me, personal growth came in the way I became more compassionate, less judgmental, and less materialistic. In all, the best thing I learned was that I am much stronger than I think. "I can do all things through Christ who strengthens me" (Philippians 4:13).

God is so good. He is my Father, my Daddy, my Papa. Unseen, He gently guides me through life, when I am often more deserving of a shove. May I learn from His example, to guide gently and unseen, so my presence is felt but not noticed.

A mission trip is a wondrous adventure with God, a magic carpet ride of discovery powered by the Almighty. Courage is needed to step out in faith onto the carpet, where our eyes can see no visible means of support. Learning to trust when we hear God's call is a giant leap of faith, rather like believing we can clear the Grand Canyon on a bicycle. See you on the other side!

Chapter Fourteen

Adventures

One summer between college semesters, Greg got a job waiting tables at a local restaurant. He and some friends wanted to go out after work, so he brought a couple of girls to the house and asked Jeff and I if we would visit with them while he took a quick shower. Of course we didn't mind, always happy to be involved in our son's life. After a few courtesies were exchanged, I asked one of the young ladies, "Now honey, do you come from a big family?" She answered, "Well, my mama is *quite large*, but my sister is thin and my brother is just average." As she was speaking I was completely lost in thought, wondering, *what on earth did I ask this girl that she would be telling me how fat her mama is?* I couldn't imagine what faux pas I could have possibly made! When I finally realized what my question was, I almost burst out laughing, but thankfully I managed to hold it in and just smiled.

When Amy was sixteen years old, she had a boyfriend named Chris. Chris helped me with a surprise birthday party for Amy by taking her to the mall shopping for her present. When he brought her home, I had twenty-five of her friends waiting in the living room. Amy walked around the corner, and everyone shouted SURPRISE! Amy was shocked! She immediately retreated to her room to collect her thoughts and gather her emotions. When I went to check on her, I could tell Amy was still a bit overwhelmed, but a big hug and a kiss on the cheek reminded her that she was greatly loved. Our sweet Amy! She just needed a bit of space to calm herself. She quickly rejoined the party and a good time was had by all.

Starting as a freshman in high school, Matthew began to develop a love for musical theater. Playing one of Ren's friends in *Footloose* was his first role. When Matthew was singing onstage, it was all I could do to refrain from jumping up on my chair and yelling excitedly, "That's my boy!" Thankfully for all involved, I was able to contain my motherly pride and just clap politely along with Jeff and the rest of the crowd.

During the summers, Matthew also performed in *Fiddler on the Roof* and Rodgers and Hammerstein's *Carousel* at St. Mary's Church. The next year S.T.M. put on *Beauty and the Beast* where Matt was egg man during the opening scene and a dancing knife in "Be Our Guest." Junior year was *How to Succeed in Business Without Really Trying* and his last play was *Charlie and the Chocolate Factory* where Matt played Mr. Salt, father of Veruca. I was very sad when Matthew took his final curtain call. It was the end of an era.

In addition to being musical, Matthew was also an athlete, joining the swim team his sophomore year. His 6'3" physique quickly went from beanpole to broad shouldered swimmer. Matt worked hard to improve, lettering in state every year. As always, Jeff and I were right there cheering him on.

When Amy was in college at LSUE, their baseball team made it to the Junior College World Series. Amy mentioned casually to her dad, "Awww, Dad! I really wish I could go to Oklahoma and watch them play." Well, Jeff made it happen for his little princess. He took a week of vacation and drove Amy and her best friend up to Enid, Oklahoma. They spent a week watching every single game. LSUE may not have won the series that year, but Amy had the time of her life. That is a memory that Amy will cherish forever, and she is devoted to baseball to this day because it reminds her of her sweet Daddy.

In the spring of 2009, I felt called to go on a pilgrimage to the Holy Land. Jeff, not a world traveler, chose to stay at home. Greg, who wanted to go with me, was now in his final year at

Loyola University New Orleans and set to graduate in May. A Finance major with a Sociology minor, Greg had already received his acceptance letter to medical school, and in no way wanted to jeopardize his future. So he went to each of his professors and posed the same question, "Will you fail me if I miss two weeks of class to go to the Holy Land with my mom, or would you be willing to work with me to make up what I miss?" Everyone agreed to work with him, so we made plans to go.

We traveled on a Footprints of God Pilgrimage with Catholic author and tour guide Steve Ray. It was incredible to see firsthand the land where Jesus walked! Visiting Bethlehem where Jesus was born, celebrating Mass in Cana where Jesus performed His first miracle – turning water into wine, and praying in Jerusalem at the site of the crucifixion of Jesus Christ was nothing short of earth-shattering. At Calvary, both Greg and I smelled the strong fragrance of roses, said to be a sign of the presence of the Blessed Virgin Mary. We stood in the Garden of Gethsemane where Jesus prayed, "My Father, if it is possible, let this cup pass from me; yet not as I will, but as you will" (Matthew 26:39). Wow. These days, I often think that exact same thought.

The pilgrimage also had a profound effect on Greg. He came home and quickly applied for a job as an escort with Steve Ray. He got the job right away and guess who was the leader and speaker on his pilgrimage? Scott Hahn, the acclaimed Roman Catholic theologian who had written the textbook that Greg had studied in his high school religion class! Internationally known speaker and author, Dr. Hahn took Greg under his wing. At every site, meal and even on the bus, Greg soaked in every word of his powerful talks and, like his mom, kept a journal of his experience. When Greg got home, he read nearly all of Scott's books, deeply absorbing everything he could about our rich Catholic heritage.

Greg then put faith into action. He formed a Catholic Bible study among his medical school classmates; so many young people yearned for spiritual growth. Next, he expanded a local branch of *Christ in the City*, an hour long service for young adults with Scripture, prayer, music, and Eucharistic Adoration followed by a social, tripling its membership. Our Holy Land pilgrimage and those two strong Catholic men provided the leadership necessary to spark in Greg a burning love for his Catholic faith. He has become quite a powerful warrior for Christ!

One sunny Tuesday when Matthew was in high school, I was visiting with Mitzi at her new house when I got a call on my cell phone. My heart leapt into my throat as I heard Matthew's voice timidly say, "Mom???" The last phone call I got from school

131

during the middle of the day ended up in an ambulance ride to the emergency room. *"Yikes!"* I wondered. *"Was something wrong?"*

Matt's gentle inquiry was followed by, "I need you to bring me some shoes and socks." … *"Ooookkkay"*…. I replied hesitantly, curious as to what condition he had arrived at school and wondering if I needed to switch to a stronger coffee bean. "The shoes I have are not uniform, and I need you to bring me another pair." *"Oh! Okay! No problem. You want your Converse? Where are they?"*

Another puzzling pause. …*I wondered what was going on. Then I heard,* "Ummm…on the roof."… *"On the roof?"* I parroted in disbelief. "Yes ma'am." *"Of our house?"* "Yes ma'am. I put them up there to dry out."

"Ooookaaaay." This conversation was getting weirder by the moment. *"Where on the roof are they, honey? At the edge?"* No ma'am. They are at the apex." I sighed deeply. *Of course they are.* Matt added, "I left them up there to dry this weekend when I was cleaning branches off the roof after the storm."

Hmmm, I thought, *fair enough.* So I weighed my options – climbing up a shaky six foot ladder with no one to hold it and scaling to the top of my house (which was growing taller by the minute), or facing the Dean of Students, a man whose entire

132

demeanor brings to mind a Fred Flintstone-like club just waiting to pound someone.

"I'll take care of it honey", I said quietly and hung up the phone.

The bewilderment on Mitzi's face while she tried to interpret this unusual one-sided conversation was hilarious. So, considering the fact that my son didn't smoke or drink, was on the honor roll, and was an Eagle Scout, I decided to take it all in stride.

I drove to my house, climbed up the wobbly ladder, and scaled the roof like an experienced mountain climber. Sure enough, just as Matt had described, there were some blue Converse shoes at the very top of our roof – dry as they could be I might add. I threw the shoes to the ground, approached the edge of the roof, and glanced down at that six foot ladder, now a half-mile beneath my outstretched foot. Gulp!

When I finally got down, I don't remember whether I kissed the ground or not, but I took a permanent marker and wrote inside the tongue of my son's shoes, **"I love my mom!"** in one shoe, and **"I have the coolest mom!"** in the other. I reasoned that with no hazardous duty pay for moms, it seemed like the next best thing. I then stuffed the shoes with a bag of gummy bears and set off to S.T.M.

When I arrived back at Mitzi's house, she didn't miss a beat. She simply asked, "Got it taken care of?", as if *everyone* had to climb up on their roof to get a pair of shoes for their child. "Yup", I replied, and we picked up our discussion right where we left off. Oh, the adventures of motherhood! There's nothing like it!

When Matthew was a junior in high school, the movie *Secretariat* was being filmed here in Lafayette, and he and hundreds of other locals applied to be an extra. Matt was in the crowd scene in the stadium during the horse race. They also chose him to be the paperboy who delivered the newspaper to the house of Secretariat's owner. Matt couldn't ride the bike *and* throw the paper directly in front of the door where they needed it, so they filmed him riding and then cut to the wheels while someone else threw the newspaper. What ended up in the movie was just Matthew's feet, but hey! That was my boy's feet! I recognized his daddy's shoes! That was a very fun and memorable experience for Matthew *and* he got paid $100 for his efforts. Matt exclaimed, "You mean I get to skip school *and* make money? This is a win-win!"

Meanwhile during the semester break at Loyola, Greg and a group of volunteers went on a three week long service/immersion trip to Belize where they taught junior high students in the morning and ran a basketball camp in the afternoon. The following year he went on a twenty-five day mission trip to Kingston, Jamaica serving the poorest of the poor in Mother Teresa's Home for the Elderly, where he visited with the destitute living there, shaved the sun-weathered faces of the old men, and trimmed their toenails. His group also worked in a children's hospital's burn ward; but before I tell you that story, I want you to know a little bit of background.

When Greg was a preschooler, he spent a week during the summer with my parents. Dad was sixty-two and Mom was fifty-eight at the time. While mom enjoyed the heck out of having Greg there, at times she needed a little down time. My dad, who was *not* good with kids and *really* not good with grandkids, *loved* Jeannie and wanted to give her a much needed break. The only thing he could think of to entertain Greg for an hour or so was to take him to the Home Depot. My elderly father and my three year old son walked hand-in-hand down every aisle, both fascinated with the vast array of gadgets. Whenever they got to the center aisle, Grandpa consulted little Greg asking, "Which way do you want to go next – left, right, or straight?"

"Hmmm" Greg pondered, "Let's go right." Home Depot can be quite an adventure for a three year old, so they continued

browsing with Greg pointing this way or that until Grandpa
finished his shopping.

Fast-forward twenty years. The children Greg encountered
in the burn unit in Jamaica were so impoverished that for a lot of
them, being in the hospital was an upgrade in circumstance; the
hospital had toys, and they had none. Greg noticed one little boy
who had bandages all over his head and both arms, so he couldn't
play with the toys. His big brown eyes peeped out sadly as he
watched the other kids play, unable to join them.

Greg, feeling compassion for the little fellow, decided to
take him walking around the hospital. Even though they didn't
speak the same language, whenever they would get to an
intersection, Greg would point and say, "Do you want to go this
way, this way, or this way?" and the little boy would say "Dis
way" and they would keep walking. When Greg took the little boy
back to the play area, his chestnut eyes were shining, proud that he
got to go on his own personal adventure!

Grandpa may have taught Greg more than we realized that
long ago day in the Home Depot. Acts of humanity never go out of
style.

Our family has been extremely blessed to have had so many life experiences. I always considered travel as part and parcel of education, and Jeff and I worked very hard to provide that for all of our children. Just as my mother took me on my first trip to Europe, it has been a blessing and an honor to in turn, take each of our children.

Greg and I went to Europe together, along with his Spanish class at S.T.M. While in Spain we went to Barcelona and Madrid, but my favorite was the ancient walled city of Toledo where we strolled its narrow labyrinth of streets and munched on freshly made marzipan cookies while we shopped. Our dip into the South of France, Monaco, and Italy only served to whet Greg's appetite for European travel. I not only got to spend time with my son, but I also bonded with my next door neighbor Mitzi, and we had more fun than the law allows. No, really! The hotel security guard knocked on our door at 3:00AM and told Mitzi and me to keep it down because we were laughing so hard it was disturbing our neighbors!

Amy and I went on a tour of Europe a few years later and saw many of the places I had seen with my mother thirty-six years earlier, and quite a few new ones. In Rome, standing in St. Peter's Square and looking at the Basilica named after our first Pope was thrilling. Standing on the Eiffel Tower overlooking the city of

Paris was breathtaking. And, we'll never forget covering almost the entire 270 acres of Kensington Gardens on foot, trying to find that darned Peter Pan statue before nightfall! Amy and I made a lifetime of memories in two weeks of travel!

The following summer, Matthew and I were on a tour of Western Canada. One day, we were eating fish and chips on the dock of the bay in sunny Vancouver; a few days later we were walking on a frigid glacier in Jasper National Park. However, the funniest thing that happened to us was on Lake Louise; two elderly ladies were staring at Matthew and giggling. Finally, they approached me and one whispered, "Is he a movie star? pointing to Matthew. Stunned, I said politely. "No ma'am. That's just my son." I should have said, *"Why yes indeedy! His feet were in Secretariat!"*

My last trip to Europe was in 2015 with Matthew. He and I enjoyed a variety of highlights everywhere we went. In Amsterdam, we toured the Anne Frank House and the Heineken Factory; whereas in Germany we cruised on the Rhine River and saw the Glockenspiel. (Watch your language!) In Venice, we wandered the twisted pathways of old and explored the Doge's Palace where Casanova famously escaped captivity from prison. One thing that surprised and enchanted us both was Isola Bella, the charming Italian island that was the home to both the magnificent palace and gardens of a noble family and a quaint fishing village. Sounds odd, but it worked! These are but a few of our wonderful memories.

Chapter Fifteen
That Fateful Fall

The last trip Jeff and I went on was to see the autumn leaves change in the Northeast. We started in Stowe, Vermont, a lovely little town where rustic covered bridges dot the landscape like stars in the sky; the Von Trapp Family Lodge provided the perfect low-key evening, complementing our laid-back day. The next morning, bright yellow and vivid orange leaves awakened our senses as we traveled through the White Mountain National Forest in New Hampshire, on our way to Freeport, Maine. There Jeff and I shopped at the L.L. Bean flagship store before heading to Kennebunkport, Maine for a juicy lobster feast.

My eyes tear up as I ponder our last few carefree days together. Staying at a nineteenth century mansion overlooking the Atlantic Ocean, Jeff and I soaked in the views. The wide front porch of the quaint old inn provided the ideal vantage point for us to watch the ocean waves hitting the black, rocky shore. Cool autumn breezes fluttered gently by, as if trying not to interrupt our conversation.

We then moved to the small restaurant inside, where a piano man played all of our favorite songs. The view of the sun hitting the ocean horizon was surprisingly emotional. Our final day of vacation was spent on the road, taking in the crimson and amber displays of God's glory, knowing that this magical world would soon disappear. On our way back to the inn, we saw our first double rainbow. Priceless!

Jeff started showing various symptoms of his illness immediately after we got home from our trip. Then, at the end of January, 2011, he fell. Further testing showed that my sweet husband had advanced brain cancer. Brain cancer, unlike any other type of cancer, attacks your mind as well as your body. It was as if Jeff had cancer, balance problems, and Alzheimer's, all at the same time.

I have a hard time remembering the events of that stressful year – perhaps I blocked them out – but I was able to dig up several old emails I had written during the year. They reminded me that the morning of Jeff's surgery, I was so sick with vomiting and dizziness that I couldn't even get up off the bathroom floor. I had to call Greg at three o' clock in the morning to drive in from his uncle's house, about 45 minutes away, and take his Dad to surgery. I was devastated that I couldn't be there with Jeff.

This is an email written two months after Jeff's diagnosis.

Hi Everyone,

I have been *very* down lately....shocked, traumatized, and hopeless. But, God is so good.

After our weekend home from Houston, spending time with all three of our precious children and cherished friends, I am re-energized! Your prayers are working. I feel *totally* filled with the Holy Spirit. I cannot explain the difference, except to say that I am now confident (which I never am), fearless (who is this woman driving all over Houston??), and joy-filled (I just have this overwhelming sense of peace about the future).

Jeff and I had a wonderful day, today. After his radiation treatment, we went to a nearby park and had a picnic, complete with sandwiches, fruit, and a decadent chocolate toffee cookie each – well actually, I had two. The sun beamed down from the French blue sky, the crisp air beckoning everyone outdoors. We sat quietly side by side at our picnic table, immersed in God's creation around us, decompressing. Blackbirds called out for their friends to join them as they rested in a stately elm tree. A delightful little squirrel sat up on his hind legs and begged for a piece of our food, which we gladly gave him; even an unusual looking creature resembling a ladybug stopped by to say hello.

But I digress. Jeff is doing really well. He is not in pain, except for a minor headache at night, and his energy level is increasing. His hair is growing back nicely from the expert haircut his brain surgeon gave him. We are striving to perceive this madness around us as a gift, and we greatly appreciate your prayers – every one of them. I know that many of you pray for us all throughout the day. Jeff and I are so grateful, and I can say, _finally_, that I can feel them. Life can be so barren without our loved ones.

Keep in touch,

Mary Ann

This next email was written at the end of April after Jeff and I got home from his six weeks of chemo and radiation.

To all our Dear Friends,

Jeff and I are now back home in Lafayette. We were greeted by a "Welcome Home" banner, balloons, and flowers. The kindness of friends who had cut our grass, tended our flower beds, and hung flowering baskets in the yard allowed us the joy of sitting outside in the sunny weekend weather, enjoying God's creation. Other sweet friends prepared meals, giving us time to rest and recuperate, enjoying our three children and the simple pleasures in life. Still others had cleaned our house from stem to stern. Every room sparkled.

A classmate of Greg's whose father was diagnosed with brain cancer five months earlier than Jeff, gave him a model car kit for Easter. The friend said that he had enjoyed putting it together with his father. Jeff and Greg spent the entire weekend bonding and sharing stories, all the while building and painting a 1968 fire engine red Ford mustang. Jeff did extraordinarily well, focusing on the minute details of the transmission, painting the tires and the rims. I was impressed!

I don't know who is happier to be home, Jeff or Spot – who had been relegated to the indignities of sleeping outdoors at his Grandmother's house. Greg gave Spot a hero's welcome home, "announcing" him into our home (game) "Starting at guard, standing thirteen inches, and weighing twenty pounds! Spot Fontenot!!!" Spot alternated the laps he slept on, so that no jealousy would abound. He spent the rest of his time on his throne-like pillow, proudly standing guard over his beloved family.

Amy and I had a girls' night out last night and went with a friend to see a movie at the picture show. That was a much needed outing.

Many thanks to everyone who sent cards or said prayers on our behalf. We are very grateful. We go back to Houston in a month for a new MRI and the results of Jeff's treatment.

God bless you one and all.

Mary Ann

Seven months after Jeff's diagnosis, I wrote this email comparing my cancer experience to Jeff's.

Hi All,
I've been encouraged to put pen to paper and share some of our journey. People have asked me, "How does Jeff's cancer experience compare to *your* cancer?" Good question. They are not even

145

remotely similar. It would be as if there were two different packages tied up in red ribbon, one containing automotive parts, the other, a frilly doll. The only commonality is the red ribbon on the outside of the package, which in this case is the word cancer.

Physically, my cancer was excruciatingly painful. With tongue cancer, every bite of food, every swallow, every moment was agonizing. Thankfully, Jeff has had little to no pain. He has a headache a few times a week which is taken care of with Tylenol.

Because I had full use of my mind and a strong will to live, I consciously availed myself of every technique known to man in order to help myself survive and enjoy quality of life. I prayed intensely, sometimes completely losing myself and being swept up into heaven – or so it seemed. I had a positive attitude (knowing that regardless of my odds, God plus one makes a majority), used visualization techniques, and had everything to live for. My life was ahead of me; I had a wonderful husband, and our children were babies, six, four, and five months old. I was determined that they would not grow up motherless. I was young – 33, strong – physically, mentally and spiritually, and absolutely in love with and trusting of our Lord. I viewed my struggles as serving a higher purpose, an opportunity for growth, growth which I dearly needed and which has served me well over the years.

Jeff, having brain cancer, is often confused, unable to recall simple things like how to get in and out of a car. It is a much more complex action than you might think. Having had a surgery where part of his brain was removed, followed by radiation and chemotherapy where the rest of it was burned and drugged, Jeff's reaction times are, understandably, delayed and his cognitive skills impaired. It all sounds horrible. It is.

Jeff turned 60 last month, is diabetic, and a bit out of shape. He gets very weak, often not being able to stand, to walk, or even to turn around. He requires round the clock, hands on, intensive care or he will fall or otherwise hurt himself. The stress on Amy and me as Jeff's caretakers is constant, compounded by our love for Jeff, fear of the unknown, grief, panic that we will do something wrong in this ever evolving situation, and complete exhaustion. Many times of the day and night, Amy and I have had to call a neighbor or even 911 to come and help us pick Jeff up when he fell on the floor, his muscles betraying his intent.

Another difference between our cancer situations were the ages of our children at the time. With the children being so young during my experience, we were able to protect them for the most part. With Jeff's cancer however, the kids are experiencing the horror of watching their beloved Dad's health and abilities decline almost weekly, as he is slowly fading away before our very eyes. It was crushing to all of us. Having to stand by and watch someone you love, struggle with a fatal disease is awful. Watching your children break down carrying that same burden is gut-wrenching.

One constant has been the overwhelming support of a loving, faith-filled community. Your love and support has been a tangible reminder that God is indeed by our side, helping us through this nightmare. The cards, emails, texts, abundance of cooked food, phone calls, visits, gifts of massages, manicures and pedicures, the four ANGELS who came while we were in Houston and cleaned our home stem to stern, even weeding our flower beds and leaving meals and other surprises around the house…it's just <u>simply unbelievable</u>. I have never felt so much love from so many.

Then, there have been the godly men placed so strategically in our lives. When a twenty-five foot limb fell in our yard inches from our roof, I stood wondering *what the heck am I going to do about this*. Well within the hour, a wonderful man from Jeff's Bible study "randomly" called saying, "I was thinking about coming to work in your yard tomorrow. Is there anything you need?" Boy was he surprised when I asked, "Do you have a chain saw?!" When he got here, he said, "You said that thing was twenty-five feet long, but I thought you were exaggerating! I was shocked when I saw how big it actually was!" However, God kept the branch from harming anyone or crushing our roof. God is good!

The men who have come by and had lunch and Bible study with Jeff, allowing him to once again be one of the gang; men who have mowed our lawn, taken Jeff out to lunch or for a snow cone, dropped by just to bring a baked chicken, or to simply sit quietly with Jeff and admire the beauty of nature…priceless.

Who can forget the musicians? The couple who came by with a guitar and played folk tunes, the barbershop quartet who came by to ring a chord with Jeff, the choir who came by to sing old church favorites, and the pianist who played hymns all brought tears to our eyes.

The gifts – how greatly appreciated were they – the CDs that kept us calm on the horrible drive to Houston, the 23rd Psalm coin that got incorporated into my prayer and journaling, the movie escapes with the girls, the lunches, the plants, the gift bags full of travel goodies, the hidden surprises.

And oh, the consolers, the listeners, the counselors – those who have kept me somewhat sane in a completely insane situation. Oh, those dear ones! When my sweet husband was diagnosed with a terminal illness, my world jumped straight into the twilight zone. My health and well-being began to decline, and I watched my children crack under the strain. My brain went on auto-pilot and events vanished from my memory as I numbed myself to the pain. I was no longer able to take in any more tragedy.

All I can say is that God's greatest gift to a human being is the love and friendship of others. There is no greater gift. For that, I thank God, and I thank you. May the peace of Christ be always with you,

Mary Ann

P.S. We have called hospice. Please keep us in your prayers. If any of you would like to come by for a visit, please do.

After he had brain surgery to remove the tumor, the Jeff we knew and loved began to disappear. It was devastating to our family – nearly breaking us – both individually and as a unit. Each of us suffered in our own unique way. The worst part of the whole ordeal was that, since we were all traumatized simultaneously, no one was able to reach out and adequately help the other. We were all drowning, side by side. Seeing my loved ones sinking and being unable to help them without losing my own tenuous grip on the life raft was brutal. My mind was simply not able to take it all in. It is only by the grace of God that I survived at all.

During the summer of Jeff's illness, at the recommendation of my spiritual director, I went to a grief seminar. I remember expressing beforehand, "I'm fine! I'm very strong! I'm perfectly okay!" Believe it or not, I really didn't think I needed help. Little did I know how much I actually did.

The day began with a prayer service, and the moment the first chord of music played, I began to sob. And I sobbed and I sobbed, and I sobbed – deep, shoulder shaking, "can't catch your breath" sobs – for a solid hour. I went through an entire box of Kleenex as my dear friend Claire sat next to me, helpless to console me. That was the only time I cried throughout Jeff's entire illness. The rest of the time, I put on a brave face and a hollow smile and did the best I could to be strong for Jeff and the kids.

Amy and I were Jeff's sole caretakers for the first six months of his illness, something I definitely don't recommend. One exception was that for the six weeks of his chemo and radiation treatments in Houston, I was with Jeff both day and night while Amy hung back with Spot to hold down the fort. When Jeff had to be hospitalized with a pulmonary embolism, thankfully

Greg was able to take off a week of med school and flew in to Houston to help me. We each took a twelve hour shift so that someone would be with Jeff day and night.

The stress of it all quickly took a toll on my body. For three months, I had shingles in my mouth. Every bite of food was excruciating, and I lost weight rapidly. Once back home, I continued to work full time. Dozens of pneumonias over the last twenty years had weakened my lungs, making it challenging to breathe. Additionally, as is true for every caretaker, I never had a day off. I was weakened and exhausted.

Ten months after his diagnosis, Jeffery Lynn Fontenot passed away on December 4, 2011. He was finally out of his pain, praise God. It was a brutal experience for our entire family – physically, mentally, emotionally, and spiritually. It is still extremely painful to think about and remains the one dark cloud in my life where I have yet to find the silver lining.

This email was written on Christmas Eve, three weeks after Jeff's death.

Dear Ones,

God is so good. He provides for us in such delicate and gentle ways. God has allowed our family the great privilege of being on His handmade beach in Destin. The sunrise beckons me to join in silent praise of our loving Creator while my children get their much needed rest. At midmorning, the sun is out in full force, but there is a cool breeze blowing. Young children race in and out of the waves, squealing with delight as they play tag with the gulf waters, oblivious to a few concealed watchers on their balconies.

My senses would argue as to which is having the best time: the view is gorgeous – the emerald water, the white sand, the simple elegance of our temporary home which Matt has rightfully called "magical". The relaxing sounds of the waves massaging the shore lull us into a peaceful sleep each night and awaken us each morning. The smell of the salt water clears my battle-weary lungs, allowing me to breathe like I once did long ago. The scents in our kitchen, – brisket and gravy, long simmered spaghetti sauce, and chicken and sausage gumbo – clamor for our attention each night, homemade dishes from kind and loving friends back home. We gratefully respond to their aroma. The feel of the sand squishing between our toes as we walk along the beach reminds us of how small we are in this picture, yet how immensely cared for. The healing conversations with visiting friends comfort our aching hearts.

Amy said that this beach trip is allowing God to heal the hole in her heart. Sitting together at lunch one day, I told Amy how soothing and calming the sound of the waves was, and that I didn't understand how or why, but that it was. My sweet angel piped up assuredly, "Well Mom, that's God! You know, in the 23rd Psalm, He says, "I will lead you beside restful waters. I will restoreth your soul." WOW, right?!

We are all getting the rest and healing we need, each in our own way.

God Bless,

Mary Ann B. Fontenot.

I wrote this poem shortly after Jeff's death.

Through the mystery of life, I awaken in a new frontier.
The immensity of God's love never wanders from my side.
I stand strong and bold in His mighty shadow.

Chapter Sixteen

Picking up the Pieces

All of my children were profoundly affected by the loss of their father, but perhaps none more than my youngest, Matthew. He was eighteen years old and just starting college when Jeff was diagnosed with cancer. Without his father's steadying presence and calming nature, Matt began to flounder both in college and in life. He changed majors a few times before finally settling into Petroleum Engineering, but Matthew finished the race, so to speak, and I could not be more proud of his hard work and determination. It may have taken him a few extra years, but my precious son persevered and graduated with a bachelor's degree in Petroleum Engineering. Matthew is now working in Lafayette and we get to see him a couple of times a week.

The summer after Jeff died, a good friend invited me to go with her on a pilgrimage to Ireland. It was an incredibly meaningful trip as I explored holy places along with my father's heritage; Dad is so Irish that he bleeds Kelly green. The striking beauty of the Irish countryside swept over my senses spreading joy to my soul. It was a delightful experience seeing so many shades of green in one vista – glorious, mind-clearing, emerald fields where the grass is so verdant that *it* is the main attraction. No flowers needed.

The Irish were friendly and talkative, like relatives I hadn't met. The numerous red haired children were like angels (and *clearly* I'm not biased at all), reminding me of my red haired, freckle-faced, Opie-looking boy back home. I used to tell Matthew that his freckles were kisses from angels who didn't want to turn him loose! It was in Ireland, wandering in solitude among sacred ruins that I learned to be a single, instead of half of a couple.

Liz Padgett is the closest thing to a sister I've ever had. Not only did we go to college together, but our children grew up together; we had ten between the two of us. Our family often joined theirs for a weekly rosary and the kids would take turns leading a decade. During the summers, Liz and I would take all of our kids to see a movie; the twelve of us would take up two rows. Greg and Amy sat in front with Sally, Renée and Stephen, while Rebecca, Sarah, Charlie, and Nicholas sat behind with Liz, Matt, and me. We called them the "big kids" and the "little kids." We also had a Christmas celebration every year. Out of our families' yearly gatherings came a very special Christmas present.

In the fall of 2012, Greg had graduated from Loyola, spent a year in the Jesuit Volunteer Corps, and was in his third year of med school while Rebecca, Liz's fourth child, had graduated from University of Louisiana at Lafayette, worked a couple of years, and done service work in Thailand. It was during this time that Greg and Rebecca finally noticed each other. Rebecca had always been one of the "little kids," and therefore not worthy of his notice.

Well, one year at our annual Christmas get together, Greg and Rebecca were thick as thieves, talking intimately, heads inches apart. Greg, Rebecca, Liz and I all remember the moment distinctly. Liz and I said to one another, "Hmm! Their heads are *awfully close.* Something's going on!" Greg remembers thinking, *Wow! This girl is kinda cute. Where has she been all my life?* Finally, Rebecca recalls thinking, somewhat indignantly, *Huh! Sally and Renée aren't here. Now Greg **has** to pay attention to me!* We all laugh about that moment.

When Greg first thought about courting Rebecca, he approached Liz and Charles and said confidently, "Dr. Charles, Mrs. Liz, you're going to be seeing a lot more of me around here because I would like to start dating your daughter Rebecca." Liz jumped up off the sofa and said, "I approve!"

Greg is now married to Rebecca, and they have two darling children: Peter, who is almost four, and Elizabeth, who is eighteen months. They are joyously expecting a third child this winter. It has really been a beautiful marriage, friendship, and relationship – a true family affair. Charles, Liz's husband, was Greg's Confirmation sponsor, and I was Rebecca's Confirmation teacher. Liz and Charles are Matthew's Godparents, and I am Nicholas' Godmother. The following are excerpts from my rehearsal dinner speech which I gave the night before my son married my best friend's daughter.

> "Liz, I've often felt that our souls were one, divided at birth and reunited in 1978 when we met in college and became the best of friends….Rebecca, I have loved you like a daughter since you were in utero, over twenty-four years ago. We became friends when you were sixteen years old, and I taught you Confirmation. I mentored you through trials and tribulations for years before you ever noticed my son, and I hope for the honor of doing that for years after."

Since Jeff died, Charles has been a surrogate father to Greg; now, he is also Greg's father-in-law. Our families are delightfully interwoven in that wonderful way that only God can pull off. That is so cool! I'm constantly impressed by God's creativity!

When Amy was twenty-four years old, we were sitting together in the Wal-Mart parking lot when I wondered aloud, "Do you think you will ever get married?" My daughter's answer was so profound that I immediately wrote it down.

"Well, maybe I will and maybe I won't, but if I do he will have to like me just as I am – you know, watching Disney movies and all – because I'm not going to change for a man" she responded proudly.

Laughing out loud, I shouted, "I *love* that spirit! *Go Amy!*" and we exchanged a high-five. To this day, Amy's self-confidence, strength of character, and fierce independence are impressive.

Matthew is what I would call an adventurer. He loves to travel and hike and just generally enjoys being in the great outdoors; he's even been spotted outside on his lunch break dozing in his blue and purple hammock strung between two trees. Matt and "Mack Attack", his five year old retired racing Greyhound that he rescued from certain death, play Frisbee in the dog park every evening before dusk. Although Matt works hard and plays hard, he is not one to stop learning. Interested in computer programming, Matt is currently taking online college courses in computer science at night.

Matthew's interest in computers and how things work began when he was in pre-school and we were at Disney World. In the "It's a Small World" ride, rather than watching all the colorfully dressed children sing, little Matthew looked down at the boat we were in, asking, "What moving us Mama? What moving us?" At four, my youngest child was observant and curious, wondering how our boat could travel through the water without oars. When I was that age, I was committing petty larceny at my father's drugstore! I'm still shaking my head over that one!

For the past few years, Matthew has been running in various races. Having completed two different half marathons, he is now training for a marathon. That opportunity will come in March, two days before his twenty-seventh birthday. One thing I do know is that if it is possible, I will be there at the finish line cheering him on. Matthew, your Dad would be so proud of you.

Greg and Rebecca bring the grandchildren over every Monday night for our family dinner. We often have wine and cheese first while visiting. One night, little Peter wandered off into the kitchen. Curious, I trailed behind. Two and a half year old Peter was eye level with the award winning cheese sitting on the table. He *really liked* that cheese! So he grabbed the whole block in his grubby little hands and held it out in front of him – gazing, salivating. Inches from Peter's fingers was our Cock-a-poo Cooper, wet nose sniffing furiously – gazing, salivating. Sensing impending doom, I thought, "*Noooooo!*" Well, I swooped in faster than a rabbit on his honeymoon, grabbed the cheese out of his hands, and cut him a slice. "*Whew!*" I thought. Crisis averted. We have fun. Tell the truth!

About twenty years after my radiation treatments ended, hastened by the stress of Jeff's illness and death, my body began to breakdown. Dr. Fields, my radiation oncologist, had warned me that the side effects of radiation would continue to build up for the rest of my life. Because the radiation that saved my life had gradually paralyzed my esophagus, I was not able to get enough nutrition by mouth, so I had to get a feeding tube.

Next, my lungs began to fail. Lacking oxygen, I would sometimes get confused or even fall in my home for no apparent reason. My salivary glands dried up so I am thirsty, day and night.

Excruciating pain was my constant companion for years. After seeing multiple doctors, I was told that my jawbone was dying from lack of blood supply, also helping explain why, for well over a year, I had been spitting out blood on a daily basis. Losing thirty pounds in the last couple of years took a toll not only my body, but also my brain. Gradually, because of lack of oxygen and proper nutrition, I lost my ability to think clearly, converse normally, read comprehensively, and write effectively. A sense of hopelessness set in.

Fear and instinct led me to seek Christ in holy places. With passports at the ready, Amy and I decided to check off one more item on my bucket list. One week later, we were on a pilgrimage to Fatima, Portugal and Lourdes, France to pray for inner peace and a sign of hope.

We flew into Lisbon, the capital of Portugal. Hours later, we went to Mass at the Basilica of St. Anthony of Padua, a place which was not even on my radar. Our tiny group of twelve celebrated Mass in this church, which honors our friend that we affectionately call Tony. The homily went something like this: "Most of us think of St. Anthony when we lose something, 'Tony, Tony, look around. Something's lost and must be found.' But St. Anthony is the patron saint of lost and desperate causes."

Hmmm. I thought. *I didn't know that, but I'm listening. Hey! I'm desperate.*

"However," the priest continued, "today I want you to think of him a bit differently. I want you to pray to St. Anthony when you *want to lose something* – like your fear or your pride…"

The homily may have continued after that point, but I just stopped listening. I couldn't believe it! What a concept! "Pray to St. Anthony to lose your fear." I was stunned. I'd just gotten off the plane a few hours ago and God was already reaching out to comfort me with a great big, God-hug. But keep listening. It gets better!

After Mass, we took a tour of the Basilica. They had a first-class relic of St. Anthony of Padua on display in a crypt where his family home once stood. What was the relic? His *jawbone*! I kid you not! I felt like God was sending me a personal message, saying, "Honey, I know what's on your mind. Let Me take that worry from you." My fear about the future left instantly, replaced with peace – that priceless Fruit of the Spirit (Galatians 5: 22-23). I said a quick prayer of thanksgiving, knowing that all is well. All is well.

Amy and I thoroughly enjoyed every moment of the pilgrimage. The weather on our ten day trip was eight cool, crisp, sunny days with blue skies and gentle breezes, and two days of cold, rainy weather in Lourdes. But you know what? It didn't dampen our spirits a bit! As a matter of fact, Lourdes was my favorite place – gray, gloomy weather and all.

I particularly loved the Basilica of Our Lady of the Rosary. That was the most beautiful church I have ever seen in my life, and Lord knows I have seen nearly a hundred of them. It was a truly sacred place. Feeling such a sense of inner peace, I couldn't help but think of my precious Mama, who would have dearly loved that Basilica. Fortunately, I was able to spend a few hours there wandering and praying among hundreds of people, yet alone with my Lord and His loved ones. I lifted up my gratitude for graces received and for faith-filled friends.

The next year, I had my third near-death experience when Matthew and I were sightseeing in Europe. We were in Switzerland at the time, high up in a mountain village, when I got altitude sickness and started vomiting. The vomiting continued intermittently for an hour, so I told Matthew, "We're going to have to call the tour director and 911. I can't breathe." It took the ambulance about thirty minutes to get up the mountain to us, so Matt and I packed quickly, with me still gasping for air.

When the two ambulance drivers arrived, they began discussing with the tour director in French whether or not my insurance would pay. Stopping that conversation short, I said urgently, "If I don't get oxygen *right now,* I am going to die." So they stopped their argument immediately, put me on the stretcher, and we all headed down to the ambulance.

By that time I was out of air and fading fast. I remember feeling the blood drain out of my face and comforting Matthew with my last breath, saying, "Honey, I love you. You will be fine, *but you have to get me home.* You will be okay. You're very strong." Holding my hand, Matthew fought back tears, his mind blown by the scene unfolding before him. Then the EMT put the oxygen on me, and suddenly I could breathe again. I felt life come back into my lifeless body.

After spending two days in a Swiss hospital with aspiration pneumonia, but a gorgeous view of the Matterhorn, Matt and I once again set out with our tour group. Life might knock me down, but it can't keep me down.

My fourth and last near-death experience occurred six months later, in November of 2015, the day before Thanksgiving. Rebecca, who was staying at her mom's house, was supposed to bring my grandson Peter over to play mid-morning. When I didn't touch base with her, Liz was alarmed, saying, "Mary Ann would *never* miss an opportunity to see Peter." She told Rebecca to call Amy and have her go check on me.

Amy walked into my bedroom and, thinking I was asleep, called out my name. "Mom? *Mom!*" Amy pleaded for me to wake up, but I was covered in sweat and unresponsive. She called Liz, and Liz said "Amy! Call 911! I'll be right over." So Liz flew over here like a bat out of hell.

The first responders arrived and couldn't get a blood pressure or a pulse, so they began CPR. My blood sugar was 19. I was not breathing, so they bagged me – forced air into my lungs – all the way to the hospital.

At the hospital, I was put on a ventilator. I was in a coma and was given the Sacrament of the Anointing of the Sick. Liz Padgett and her entire family joined my children in praying a rosary in the chapel. That night, I was so close to death that Greg cautioned his sister, "Amy, the doctors don't think Mom will make it through the night, so you need to prepare yourself for that."

The next day, my friend Liz Hill was by my side praying the rosary for me. This is what she later told me,

"In the middle of the rosary, I stopped and said urgently, 'Mary Ann! I just don't know what to pray for! I don't know if you want to live or die!'

Liz continued her story with tears in her eyes, "At that moment, you came out of the coma, and with a strength I didn't even know you had, grabbed me by the collar and said, '*Fiiiight!*' From that point on, you started recuperating."

My family and I decided that I would get a tracheostomy, so that I could get off of the ventilator. After several days in the hospital, I was discharged to a Long-Term Acute Care Hospital for three more weeks before being released. I got home two days before Christmas. Hallelujah! God is good!

Recovery was a year-long journey of physical therapy, speech therapy, and grit. Many virtues were painstakingly honed. For some reason, thanks to God and His mysterious ways, I beat the odds yet again. Perhaps it was to write a book?

Chapter Seventeen

A Tribute to Amy

My Dad often tells me that I am his hero. Well, my hero is my daughter, Amy Lynn Fontenot. Amy has had to struggle all of her life. What may have come easily to some children was an uphill battle for Amy. She didn't begin crawling until she was fourteen months, so our pediatrician referred us to a specialist in New Orleans. That doctor ordered a M.R.I. of her brain to figure out what the problem was.

I dressed Amy up in her beautiful, red, Christmas dress, so she would feel special. We headed for the hospital. Seeing my baby girl laying on the M.R.I. table with nothing but her black, patent leather Mary Jane's, and her white, ruffled ankle socks sticking out of that huge machine, broke my heart. It was the saddest sight I'd ever seen.

Jeff and I met back with the doctor for the results of the scan. She told us that Amy had, among other things, "developmental delays of unknown origin which will last a lifetime." From the moment those words came out of the physician's mouth, I went into shock. The thought of our little girl having such major challenges ahead of her for the rest of her life was overwhelming to me. I couldn't believe it! Sick to my stomach, I went home and climbed straight into bed. I began shaking uncontrollably and couldn't stop trembling for about fifteen minutes. I was so scared. Jeff looked on helplessly and tried to comfort me by covering me with my favorite blanket, but a blanket is no match for fear.

The next day, I was scheduled to work in Lake Charles, over an hour's drive from home. Determined to honor my commitment, I drove the entire way in silence with our precious daughter on my mind. Fifteen minutes after beginning my shift, I started crying and was completely unable to compose myself. Twenty minutes later, still crying, I called the scheduler, who sent a pharmacist to replace me.

The drive home was torturous. My mind raced with thoughts. What will Amy's life be like? Did I do something to cause this? Can our family handle this challenge? When I got home, I spent the rest of the morning lying in bed in a darkened room. Like most mothers, I thought, *surely there is something I can do to fix this problem. Surely, I can make it better....surely so.*

Jeff and I put Amy into occupational therapy twice a week and began striving to increase her mobility by helping her practice her gross motor skills (arms and legs), and fine motor skills (fingers and hands.) She had delays in both. Not only did Amy need to learn a whole new set of skills, like walking and using her pincher fingers, but Jeff and I had to learn to parent differently. We were both up for the challenge.

Making use of my love of reading, I once again hit the library and checked out every book on how to help children with disabilities – learning and otherwise. Amy didn't walk until she was almost two years old and had similar struggles in school. In the third grade, she was diagnosed with multiple learning disabilities and struggled academically from that point on.

Now, Amy is doing incredibly well. Wise beyond her years, Amy freely admits that she is a much stronger person because of all the challenges she has gone through. With relentless hard work and optimism to spare, Amy has exceeded all expectations. She learned to drive when she was twenty-one years old and hasn't looked back since! Loved by all who know her, Amy really is the little engine that could.

The thing that helped me the most to get a feel for raising a child with a learning disability and developmental delays is this wonderful story written in 1987 by Emily Pearl Kingsley. It changed my perspective on the situation and helped me adjust my thinking and adapt to a new normal.

"Welcome to Holland"

By: Emily Pearl Kingsley

I am often asked to describe the experience of raising a child with a disability – to try to help people who have shared the unique experience to understand it, to imagine how it would feel. It's like this…

When you're going to have a baby, it's like planning a fabulous vacation trip – to Italy. You buy a bunch of guidebooks and make your wonderful plans. The Coliseum, Michelangelo's David, the gondolas in Venice. You may learn some handy phrases in Italian. It's all very exciting.

After months of eager anticipation, the day finally arrives. You pack your bags and off you go. Several hours later, the plane lands. The stewardess comes and says, "Welcome to Holland."

"Holland!" you say. "What do you mean, Holland? I signed up for Italy! I'm supposed to be in Italy. All my life I've dreamed of going to Italy."

But there's been a change in the flight plan. They've landed in Holland, and there you must stay.

The important thing is that they haven't taken you to a horrible, disgusting, filthy place, full of pestilence, famine, and disease. It's just a different place.

So you must go out and buy new guidebooks. And you must learn a whole new language. And you will meet a whole new group of people you have never met.

It's just a different place. It's slower paced than Italy, less flashy than Italy. But after you look around; you begin to notice Holland has windmills, Holland has tulips, Holland even has Rembrandts.

But everyone you know is busy coming and going from Italy, and they're bragging about what a wonderful time they had there. And for the rest of your life, you will say, "Yes, that's where I was supposed to go. That's what I had planned."

The pain of that will never go away because the loss of that dream is a very significant loss.

But… if you spend your life mourning the fact that you didn't get to Italy, you may never be free to enjoy the very special, the very lovely things…about Holland.

Amy is just fine. The love and time that Jeff and I invested into our precious daughter, and her perseverance, hard work, and positive attitude is the story of a winner. It is the story of a little girl who believed in herself because her family believed in her. We told her she could!

Today, Amy has a job with a great company, lives at home with me, and is very involved in our church. Between ball games, going to the movies, and our family get-togethers, she stays busy and always has a smile on her face. Amy is an enormous help to me as my health declines, and I thank God every day for sending me an angel.

Chapter Eighteen

Reflections

Growing up, everything in my life was stable. I had one house as a kid, one job as a teenager, and one career as an adult. After working at my dad's pharmacy for ten years, I then worked at Eckerd Drugs/CVS for thirty years until I retired. Pharmacy has changed tremendously over forty years. I remember when ibuprofen, the very first non-steroidal anti-inflammatory drug, (N.S.A.I.D.) hit the market. There was a mad frenzy among our customers as supply couldn't keep up with demand. Old ladies suffering with arthritis would beg my dad to save them some. Now, there is an entire pharmacy aisle devoted to pain relievers.

I grew up in a quiet, picturesque little town which had the best life had to offer. Culture and education were highly valued in Covington, and crime was very low. Life was wonderfully slow-paced. When I moved to Lafayette after college, I once again got the best of both worlds. Big enough to have cultural and educational events yet small enough to feel a sense of community, Lafayette is the perfect place for me.

A good example of the sense of community that Lafayette has was when Amy was driving to the salon to get her hair cut and got a flat tire. Amy called Mitzi for help since she lived nearby, but Mitzi was out of town. She told Amy to bring her car to Sterling at Delta World Tire. Mitzi then called Sterling and explained that Amy may not have enough money in her checking account to cover a new tire, so she asked him to put it on her husband, Frankie's account. Next, Amy called her hairdresser, Kellie Landry, and told her she was going to be late for her hair appointment. Kellie, a feisty little blonde that we've been going to for years, was so worried about Amy on that busy street that she told Amy, "I can change a tire. I'll be right there."

So Kellie, 5'4"and all of 110 pounds soaking wet, set out in her navy blue dress and high heels to help my daughter change her tire. Well, then the River Ranch mailman, Gerald, saw two women in distress and was gentlemanly enough to pull over and lend a hand. A passerby, impressed with the mailman's kind gesture, took a picture of the scene and posted it on Facebook as a hometown hero. Then Amy drove to see Sterling and he gave Amy a new tire and didn't charge her a dime! He even refused payment from Frankie. He was just a nice man doing a good deed.

They say it takes a village – well, I believe Lafayette is a village – a village of warm, friendly, good-hearted, people. I have no doubt that when I'm long gone, Amy will still have a thousand guardian angels!

176

My first Bible Study was a year after my initial cancer diagnosis. I had never studied the Bible before, but now, I found I couldn't read anything *but* the Bible. I immersed myself in it for twenty years, taking almost fifty different in-depth studies. Somewhere along the line, I heeded the call for Confirmation teachers at church, shifting my focus to the next generation. The opportunity to witness my faith to young people who were just solidifying their own was incredibly meaningful to me. Feeling it was part of my mission, I dove headfirst into winning souls for Christ. Yes, there were those I couldn't reach, but I planted a lot of seeds which produced a lot of fruit.

Some examples of the seeds that took root are: One Sunday after church, a couple came up to me and the mother said, "You *saved* our son! He was on a very bad path before the Confirmation classes started, and you really helped turn him around." I was overjoyed to hear that! I had no idea. Many students of mine went on to lead student ministry. They felt like my own kiddos! One young lady, a student of mine from five years earlier, came up to Amy at Chick-fil-A and told her, "Your mom was the best religion teacher I ever had! She helped me apply faith to life." Wow! Those stories are very gratifying to hear!

I'm so grateful that God allowed me the privilege of raising my children until they were grown.

Greg, I am extremely proud of the fact that you and Rebecca have chosen not to have a television in your home. I'm certain it has its challenges, but the benefits are vast. The relationships nourished between husband and wife, parent and child will pay off in spades over the long haul. In the meantime, you have two flourishing gardens, and your family lives off the land.

Amy, now that you're a Eucharistic Minister at Holy Cross Church, nothing brings me more joy than receiving Christ through my child. I'm thrilled that you are settled and have sixty new friends from the A.C.T.S. retreat (Adoration, Community, Theology, and Service). I'm happy that you stay so active; your singing in the choir is the cherry on top!

Matthew, you are a strong, confident man with an unparalleled work ethic, and I couldn't be more proud of you. You always land on your feet, no matter the circumstances, and that quality will get you far in life. You definitely inherited your Dad's singing ability! Perhaps you will join a barbershop quartet someday.

So what is life like for me now? Well, with my feeding tube in, I used to miss eating until my coma put everything in perspective. Gratitude replaced cravings. I have a trachestomy and a paralyzed vocal cord so I have difficulty speaking, and because of my decreasing ability to breathe, I am now on oxygen 24/7. (More on that later.) I was in constant pain for several years until I started a new treatment which has finally alleviated the pain. Thank you, God! After spitting out blood daily for well over a year, I was diagnosed with a bone infection in the radiated area of my jaw. My last hope is the six weeks of I.V. antibiotics that I just completed. If that doesn't work, there is nothing else that can be done. At best, it's only a temporary fix.

My disfiguring scars have never bothered me because I decided a long time ago that I would rather be horribly disfigured than the prettiest girl in the graveyard. My scars are my red badge of courage!

Being low on oxygen does a lot of interesting things to both your mind and your body. Amy told me that the summer before my coma, she and I went to a Garth Brooks concert. I had no recollection of that. Now, how the heck can you not remember a Garth Brooks concert? Is that even possible? I still remember Jeff

179

and me attending our first Garth concert almost thirty years ago, where he swung across the stage on a rope! Well, as Amy talked me through our concert experience, I slowly recalled going. *My* memory of it was of being in terrible pain the entire time, and being unable to breathe because our seats were up in the nose-bleed section. But Garth came to New Orleans, and my daughter wanted to go, so I took her. Amy had the time of her life, and that's all that matters.

I don't remember much from the months before my coma, but here is one thing I do remember. Although I had my feeding tube by that time and couldn't eat, Amy wanted to try out a local dessert restaurant, so we went. It was mid-August and so hot and muggy in there that I couldn't breathe. This was before I realized my lungs were failing and got my portable oxygen.

Well, the weirdest thing happened! I was talking to Amy, and then everything went black. Amy saw me lose consciousness and immediately shook my arm and said, "Mom! You fell asleep!" I quickly realized that I had just passed out; however, I didn't understand that this was a permanent situation. I just knew that something was terribly wrong with my body and it was incredibly frightening. My brain couldn't make sense of it all. After my coma, when I was finally put on oxygen 24/7, I gradually recovered my ability to read, a privilege I do not take for granted. No oxygen? No bueno!

All things considered, I realize that everyone has their burdens to carry, but for me the gifts of life and faith tip the scale in my favor. So many people didn't have the privilege of raising their children to adulthood. Once I re-evaluated my life with the perspective of eternity, then my load seemed a whole lot lighter. I rarely worry about the future because I've learned that when I worry, I am envisioning a future without God in it. Things have rarely turned out as bad as I had imagined they would be, because when their time came, God walked me through them. God has boundless strength to carry us and delightful surprises hidden along the way. All we have to do is trust Him.

Over the years, many people have told me that I have a "great sense of peace about me" and "a graceful acceptance of my disabilities." Please know that it didn't come overnight and it didn't come easily. Like the Apostle Paul, I begged the Lord to take away my disabilities, my struggles, my pain, and like Paul, the answer I received was "My grace is sufficient for you, for my power is made perfect in weakness" (2 Corinthians 12:9).

In the beginning, I was terribly ashamed of my frailty and differences. However, with prayer, time, and the love of family, friends, and a vibrant Catholic community, I began to change my way of thinking. I had to make friends with my weakness. Like my friend, Kally, says "It's an opportunity for others to step up and help, and sometimes they need that." I believe with all my heart that God's grace *is* sufficient for me. He has assured me that it is.

My prayer life is very active; I raise my thoughts to God often, in praise, thanksgiving and petition. I've found if I can slow my breathing, relax my body, and clear my mind, my prayer life explodes. In that way, I am allowing God the space necessary for a response. Sometimes I think that God is not answering my prayers, but it may be that He can't get a word in edgewise!

The peace I have now comes directly from a close relationship with Jesus Christ in prayer. I turn to Him daily for strength, hope, and guidance. I am not a goody two-shoes. I am not holier than thou. I am simply a woman who fell head over heels in love with Jesus Christ. Like with any other love relationship, I wanted to know more and more about my Beloved – the Man who changed my life forever – so I immersed myself in Scripture. The more I learned about Him, the more I wanted to know; I simply couldn't get enough.

Learning to trust God, and discovering the peace that comes with that trust, is a process. Again, it's like any other relationship. I gained it in small, daily doses over the last twenty-six years.

My friend Kally once told me, "The word trust implies that we don't know what's in our future. If we knew, then it would be called preparation. Trust implies that we don't know; however, we know who does, and that is God."

The peace I have does indeed transcend all understanding. The road to that peace may have been an uphill climb with a backpack full of rocks, but I've always enjoyed the view. I never felt God owed me anything; I never felt that God abandoned me either. God was by my side every step of the way, even in stormy weather.

I've found that gratitude opens the door for blessings to enter our lives. Once we are grateful for what we have, rather than focusing on what we don't have, the door opens for peace, love, and joy to flow in. The only time I ever looked at my body and loved what I saw was when scars were covering it. I was so grateful to be alive! Facing death at 33 and having to make plans for my children that didn't include me, ushered in the most peaceful moment in my life. I was so grateful to have a strong faith which reassured me that my Heavenly Father was waiting for me. On my mission trip to Mexico, I renewed my gratitude for the basic essentials of life, having seen up close and personal so many who lived without.

Cancer will either make you bitter, or it will make you better. I chose better. Cancer may have been the worst thing that ever happened to me, but it was also the best thing that ever happened to me. It taught me to appreciate every moment – even the bad ones – and to look for the silver lining in every disappointment or tragedy.

Along the way, I got my PhD in pain, I was summa cum laude in suffering, and I got my doctorate in discomfort. However, our God is loving and kind, gracious and merciful; with all of the pain and disabilities that He blessed me with, He also gave me a priceless yet undeserved gift. God gave me the gift of indescribable joy: the joy of being able to help others, the joy of being used by God, *the joy of knowing that my unique experience means something to the Creator of the Universe!* **And yours does, too**.

Tidbits of Wisdom

All of my life I have loved wisdom and been irresistibly drawn to those who have it. Wisdom, like purity, is endlessly attractive. Wisdom is eternal. My mother, Jeanne, the epitome of purity and virtue, told me when I was a child, "I may not always like *what you do*, but I'll always love *you*." In that simple statement, she taught me to separate the child from his behavior. You can love the child *and* find his behavior unacceptable. That also taught me an important lesson about God and His relationship with us, His children.

Some of the other things Mom taught me were:

Advice is free. Always take it. You don't have to *use* it, but always *take* it.

If you can't say something nice, don't say anything at all.

If he will cheat *with you* on someone else, he will cheat *on you* with someone else.

Always put Band-Aids and M&Ms in your Christmas stockings.

It's better to keep your mouth shut and have people *think* you're stupid, than to open your mouth and remove all doubt.

Dad taught me many things as well such as:

Everything we have is a gift. God owes us nothing. If we have our eyesight, our health, friendships, love, a job – all of those are gifts. If you have a hot shower and a cold glass of water, appreciate it. These are things many people don't have.

Life is not supposed to be fair.

Always give people the benefit of the doubt.

Apologize when you are wrong and say the words, *"I am sorry for…"* naming what it was that you did wrong, loudly and clearly. Taking ownership of our mistakes keeps us humble. As kids, Dad always made us apologize to Mom after we got punished.

Give a man a hard day's work for his money and you'll never be out of a job.

From Jeff, I learned the importance of memorizing Scripture. That simple lesson still benefits me many years after his death.

He also said, "You can never out give the Lord." I've found that to be true.

When I was fresh out of college, Jeff told me "You can find something worth complimenting in everyone." Wise words.

Some tidbits of wisdom I learned from experience are:

After love, the most important trait in good parenting is *consistency*. You must be consistent.

Realize that some people may need to talk more than we need to listen. At times, being a good person involves listening to the same old stories over and over again, simply for the joy it gives the speaker. God blesses us through that activity. It allows Him to develop our patience and character.

We notice the flaws in others that most closely resemble our own.

If you want to see a behavior to be repeated, pay attention to it.

Learning the difference between urgent and important revolutionized my life. Urgent things have a deadline. With important things, time is not a factor.

We do our children a disservice if we buffer them from consequences. It is consequences that cause change.

It's important to have a device free day once a week.

God creates! Look at your loved ones – that's pretty impressive!!

We are stronger than we think.

"Joy is not the absence of trouble but the presence of Christ."

Pain is a powerful motivator for change.

Encouragement sustains life.

Final Thoughts

My life is a gentle interweaving of faith and times gone by. Confronted time and again by the imminent prospect of loss of life, death no longer has a hold on me. As my dear ole Dad likes to say, "There are worse things in life than dying." I have managed to come to grips with a severe loss of ability while still helping others along the way, thus giving my suffering purpose. At first, my greatest challenge was recognizing my own frustrating limitations and changing my self-image from a strong, confident, vibrant woman, to one who must accept help from others. That was incredibly difficult for me because I'd always prided myself on being self-sufficient; I, after all, was the one who helped others.

After my coma, my challenge became lifting my self-image from a weak, broken, person to a strong, whole survivor who carries on regardless of circumstances. My body may fail me at times, but my soul thrives! Twenty-six years after a near fatal cancer, I still make it to church on Sunday and can play with my darling grandchildren. If I had not been guided by the wisdom of my mother and toughened by the steel of my father, I would not be alive today. I am indeed blessed.

To my precious children, Greg, Amy, and Matthew, please know this: Parenting is life's ultimate challenge. I did the best I could, with what I had at the time. I urge you to stay close to the Lord. You never know when you will need His help and you'll want to be on speaking terms. Enjoy each other. Help each other. Stay close, *no matter what it takes*. Blood is thicker than water. You can never replace blood. Most of all, remember I love you.

This is a poem I wrote while grieving after Jeff died.

All of nature is sacred ground, life itself created for our joy and fulfillment. Blessed wisdom can be gained from the earth.
Trees heal broken hearts.
Birds soothe frazzled nerves.
Flowers lift wounded spirits.
The holy combination of nature and solitude invoke the tranquility and peace yearned for from the beginning of time.

36229381R00120

Made in the USA
Middletown, DE
12 February 2019